★ RISE

In Pursuit of Empowerment

Many Blessings Faith Rodriguez

INTRODUCED BY ★ SABINE MATHARU

This book has been written for information purposes only.
Every effort has been made to make this book as complete
and accurate as possible.

However, there may be mistakes in typography or content. Also, this
book provides information only up to the publishing date. Therefore, it
should be used as a guide – not as the ultimate source. The purpose of
this book is to educate.

The author and the publisher do not warrant that the information
contained in this book is fully complete and shall not be responsible for
any errors or omissions. The author and publisher shall have neither
liability nor responsibility to any person or entity with respect to any
loss or damage caused or alleged to be caused directly or indirectly
by this book.

For bulk order email: **contact@reachforgreatness.co.uk**

Copyright

Title book: RISE - In Pursuit of Empowerment
Author: Sabine Matharu

Dedicated to my amazing husband Pritpal
and my 2 children Sasha and Sarina
who are my love and joy,
and give me purpose and inspiration.

This book has been "given to me as a mission"
to help women "RISE" and tell their stories.
Through this beautiful project, we are sharing
encouragement and wisdom when it comes to
facing our every day challenges in life.

"Let's Reach For Greatness together."

- Sabine Matharu -

★ FOREWORD ★

For some of us, reaching for greatness comes from a choice,
a moment in time when a decision is made to take a step forward.
For others, greatness is simply showered upon us as a result of the
decisions we have made and the actions we have taken.

For me, I have witnessed greatness in an entirely different way.
I have seen greatness manifest in the consistent, daily action of
showing up and being true to oneself. Greatness has shown itself in the
commitment to a vision, which one is unwilling to let go of.

In this book of wisdom and discovery, not only will we read the
empowering stories of greatness shared, but we are also witnessing
the greatness of one woman holding true to her vision.

Like many of us, Sabine started her professional journey feeling
stuck and truly feeling the weight of her business. Through this,
she wilfully persevered, trying to do things the way she expected
they should be done. When Sabine finally gave herself permission to
trust her intuitive self and to reach for greatness in her life, the magic
began to filter through. It was then, when she focused connecting with
other women, embracing her gifts and helping those around her
to experience their greatness, that she too learned to reach for
her greatness within herself.

This publication is in fine company alongside Sabine's
other passions "Greatness T.V" and "The Greatness Club",
which she has nurtured soulfully and completely,
to make them the successes which they are today.

Reaching for greatness comes in so many different forms,
as we will observe within the powerful stories in this book.
Having had the privilege of being one of Sabine's most significant
mentors during her beautiful journey,
I have been fortunate to watch her continuously
take steps forward toward her unfaltering vision.

A woman of integrity, love and true tenacity, Sabine has grown
and flourished on her way to greatness,
whilst sharing the magic she has within her.
Magic which brings people together. Magic which empowers.

As we all strive to reach for that next level of greatness in our careers,
in our businesses and in our personal lives,
I am sure that these stories will inspire you,
whilst reminding you of what is truly possible
when you choose to believe and take that first step.

I wish Sabine a huge congratulations on taking this incredible
leap on her journey to greatness.

- *Claire Macpherson* -
Unleashed business growth coach for women ready for more!

★ REVIEWS ★

There's always a deeper reason why entrepreneurs do what they do. I think when women in particular, are driven to create businesses that make a difference to the world, their unique stories of personal growth, their struggles and their burning desire for fulfilment reflects a quest for wholeness in their lives with which other women can all resonate. Sabine has done a beautiful job bringing together these themes in 'Rise'. Each woman featured in the book has her individual story and there is a collective atmosphere of positivity, determination and vision that makes this an inspiring, uplifting and honest read.

- Rhian Kivits -

Love & Intimacy Mentor

When you look around you and often feel envious of other women who seem to be 'making it', speaking on stages, making an impact and enjoying financial success, it's too easy to believe that somehow, they got luckier, or are smarter than you, or braver, or more confident. The truth about what it takes to breakthrough to greatness is quite different.

'Rise' is a compendium of inspirational stories that will confirm to you that you are right where you need to be. 'Rise' will have you turning the pages of 25 women's true stories of how they overcame all the odds to reach their success prizes. Blood, sweat, tears, grief, poverty, hard work and persistence are what it takes to truly rise to one's greatness, and 'Rise' will have you feeling "I am one of those ladies, I can do this too!" Human stories are the real truth behind success. This little gem will warm your heart and light your fire!

- Jenni P -

Iconic Life Connoisseur, Mentor for Creative Myth Makers

From start to finish this book had my attention. I was eager to read more about these courageous women who dared to face their challenges and rise above their circumstances to make a positive impact, not only on their own life, but to the lives of others. MIND BLOWN!

- Gia Lili -

Love and Relationship Coach

I'm so grateful to each lady who shared her story in this incredible collection - each one is magnificent! I was hooked and totally inspired, uplifted and empowered. I recommend this book to all my clients, friends and family.

- Christine King -

Life Magic Coach

What can I say about this book 'Rise'. Each story is an amazing journey, which gives you hope. Each of these amazing ladies, are all heroes and have overcome their own individual circumstances to move forward, in the pursuit of their dreams while serving the greater good.

The captain of the ship, Sabine Matharu, shares her own amazing journey from the corporate world to becoming an entrepreneur. Each story is both uplifting and entertaining. If you are in need of some motivation, want to gain courage to pursue your dreams, to rise out of your current circumstances, then this is the book for you. It will fill your heart with courage and passion to go out and live your life on your terms and make your dreams a reality.

- Gull Khan -

Money Mindset Expert

★ PREFACE ★

I would like to say thank you to my family who have supported me
throughout my entrepreneurial journey. My colleagues, friends, my mentors
and all the amazing women that have come together to
co-author this fabulous book and who share parts of their life journey

I am a passionate business start up and growth strategist and specialise in supporting women to find their purpose and monetise their unique skills to help them build thriving businesses. I do this by teaching them step by step business strategies along with balancing work and life priorities. Having had years of experience as a corporate trainer, I was fortunate enough to have coached and worked with over 1000 people in leadership positions. When I started my own business, I fell into the trap of being overwhelmed. I had lost my way, didn't feel aligned and hence had no results to show for. With my back against the wall, I managed to turn things around within the space of 90 days and I got off to a flying start. For many years I had been sowing the seeds and now I was ready, all my ideas started to flourish, received amazing feedback and I got myself fully booked within weeks.

When I first started in business, I had always dreamt of having a space where I felt I would be part of a family as opposed to being a lonely entrepreneur working from home, where I did not get any feedback, feeling frustrated, not knowing what my next steps would be and how to create results in my business. I craved an inspirational environment that was personal and helped women implement step by step and receive real time feedback in relation to their progress and next steps. So the "The Business Accelerator Mastermind" was born, where I develop and nurture entrepreneurial women closely to achieve the success they deserve. A safe space where I not only coach them on cutting edge strategy and technology, but also develop friendships and have a chance to exchange ideas, get support and accountability as we implement.

Secondly, I also run "The Greatness Club", which helps women with growth, visibility and creating collaborative opportunities.

There are 3 key principles:

Growth

Every month we implement 1 business topic in detail, which consists of a Workshop, Workbook, Expert Q&A and sharing progress.

Visibility

Monthly online 'Speed Networking' events allow us to connect with potential clients where we are able to present what we do in business.

Reach For Greatness TV and the Greatness Magazine gives Club members a chance to become visible through being a contributor.

Community

Through Expert Q&As, I invite guest speakers into the Club on a monthly basis to provide quality training that can also lead to further collaboration with Club members.

The Greatness Stories are a series of books which help women entrepreneurs share how they overcame their struggles and challenges, and help other women to find hope and courage.

You can get more information about the community and my programmes as well as special offers by singing up for the book bonuses on the next page.

Lastly, with everything I do at Reach For Greatness, it's about helping women create a balance in life and business, achieve their full potential and live their greatness as well as helping charitable organisations that are in need of funding. You will find the charities we support in the back of this book. In this way, we can do good together on a number of levels.

- Sabine Matharu -
Founder of Reach for Greatness

RISE

In Pursuit of Empowerment

GRAB YOUR BOOK BONUSES TODAY

Fabulous bonuses have been selected for our gorgeous readers that will support you on the journey to Greatness in your personal and business growth.

Please follow the link below.

★ **www.learnmoreabout.info/rise** ★

★ CONTENTS ★

"When you release your magic,
you light up the path for others."

- Sabine Matharu -

REACH FOR GREATNESS

Born and raised in Austria, I was conditioned to go to school, work, marry and have children. This was considered a normal, well lived life of the average Austrian at the time I was being raised. However, for as long as I can remember, there was something intuitive telling me that I was born to do more. I was by nature, an adventurous child, who spent most days outdoors, playing in the woods and even sowing the seeds for entrepreneurship. One day during the summer holidays, I sparked off an idea to sell home-made stationary at the side of the road to by-passers. My arts and crafts skills were probably not up to scratch, and at the time I really didn't care. Looking back, it was a bit of fun, however the biggest lesson was that I allowed myself to be free and I truly 'went for it' without fear of failure or being judged.

Fast forward a few years, I completed my university degree. Seeking out yet another adventure, I packed my bags and headed to the United Kingdom. With stars in my eyes, hope in my heart and joy in my bones, it felt like I was finally putting on my 'big girl' boots and taking on the world. With a good qualification in my hands and a thousand pounds in my pocket, I was sure that it wouldn't take long for me to find a decent, well paying job. Thoughts of a bright future and visions of me prospering warmed my heart.

The anticipation was wonderful, almost like being in love. With all these positive vibrations, what could possibly go wrong?

As soon as I arrived, it was clear that my thousand pounds was not going to see me through. Settling for accommodation that was way below the standard I was accustomed to, a youth hostel where I lived with 18 others and a couple of rats, was the only option.

I consoled myself with the thought that I would begin the job hunt immediately to be able to move on quickly. My bubble burst when I faced rejection repeatedly. To top it all, there were no friends or family to rely on to support me, hence I had to navigate my way around the city by myself. At this rate, the possibility of running out of money before finding a job was very high. Nonetheless, I persevered and told myself that going back to seek help from my parents was not an option. I wanted to show the world that I could master anything that life threw at me.

My perseverance paid dividends. After finally finding a decent job through sheer determination, things were on the rise and falling into place, as I was introduced to my future husband through a work colleague. Building momentum and working my way up the corporate ladder, things couldn't have been any better, when I was offered my 'dream' position in management consulting. I was excited as I was travelling a lot to see clients, lived out of suitcases, and went from hotels to boardrooms and back to the airport again. During that time I was training hundreds of people, influencing their lives in positive ways and I absolutely loved it!

There were many moments in my career and life, when I lived on an absolute high, believing that nothing could ever overpower those feelings. I was so wrong. Every woman will tell you that nothing compares and is more invincible than the feeling of becoming a mother. It changed my life completely. Whereas, I always felt that I would give birth and return to work after my maternity leave, I was least prepared for the overwhelming feeling that nothing was more important than my child and wanting to be there for him.

Eventually I went back to work and soon got into the swing of things, at times feeling guilty for not being there for my son as he was just a little toddler. When I had my second child, those old feelings of wanting to be there for the both of them now, returned.

Being used to creating new and exciting things, I took the plunge and used my skills to open my own business as a leadership and coaching consultant.

A few years later, realising that there was a whole new world when it comes to expanding my business online, I ventured into yet a new arena that was initially overwhelming. Learning everything about starting and growing a business using the internet and social media, sadly my path consisted of many 'shiny objects', pitfalls and unnecessary detours.

For me, this was the turning point. I remembered how playful and 'free spirited' I was as a child. So it dawned on me, that my mission was to create a platform for women entrepreneurs, to help them reduce the overwhelming challenges of starting and running a business, avoiding costly mistakes and detours. This is when I decided to launch "Reach for Greatness".

Within the space of 3 years, it has developed into a thriving platform that integrates "The Greatness Club" as well as an exclusive Mastermind, called "The Business Accelerator". Women learn to develop their entrepreneurial skill set and strategies to implement and run a successful business at various levels. My programmes also focus on creating a balance between business and personal growth, supported by collaborate opportunities to become more visible. This series of books was inspired by this vision.

Whilst what I do in "Reach for Greatness" delivers transformational breakthroughs in business, it is also my desire to help others by being approachable, caring and compassionate. I believe, helping those that are less fortunate to become empowered, to create sustainable and balanced lives for themselves, is the greater part of my legacy and will live on even when I am no more.

SABINE MATHARU

BUSINESS START UP & GROWTH STRATEGIST

reachforgreatness.co.uk

Sabine Matharu is a passionate business start up and growth strategist, who specialises in helping women find their purpose and monetise their unique skills so that they can build a thriving business.

Her signature program is "The Business Accelerator Mastermind", that teaches and supports entrepreneurs to implement an easy to follow methodology around how to build a long term profitable business without overwhelm and detours.

She also runs "The Greatness Club", which complements the work she does in her Mastermind and provides women a platform and springboard for visibility, networking and lead generation.

Sabine comes with years of experience as a corporate leadership consultant and has worked with over 1000 people in senior positions.

She firmly believes that it is possible to reach for the greatness that is within ourselves.

"You all have the right to reclaim what has been muted, oppressed or ignored by others and by yourself. Never deny the power of your voice. The world needs to hear what you have to say."

- Nadine Barrett -

FROM SEGREGATION & SILENCE TO FINDING MY VOICE

They said I was an introvert. Maybe I was born that way or maybe it was life itself that taught me that it was safer to distance myself from the world and look within.

Imagine feeling ignored because you were too gentle to scream for what you wanted. Imagine a little girl, forced to identify herself as different, because the colour of her skin made some men and women react with utter disgust. Imagine being born in a place you call home but still being a stranger to it because you sounded different to the world surrounding it.

Of course, I appear today to be a confident, accomplished woman and I am, however few know what it took to get to this point. How often do we truly stop to consider the journey that someone else has taken to get to the point that we met them at? We all have a story to tell and this is a part of mine.

Over 20 years ago, I should have been engrossed in playing hopscotch at school or deciding which teddy bear or pony was my favourite. Instead I was burdened with existing in a hostile, life threatening environment. I was a perceptive child, a deep thinker and understood the world around me in exceptional detail.

So, I knew the situation had reached a critical point when even my passive, peace loving father started fighting his way home from work, because the looks and insults had been swapped for weapons and physical attacks.

At school, there were always insulting remarks, a lack of understanding about me and an annoying invasion of my personal space when kids reached in to grab my hair. I quickly toughened up to assert the fact I was not some toy to be played with or asked the same old stupid questions over and over again. Some other kids got the message and kept their distance. It was clear to me that ignorance was a big problem.

What was not okay, was for racist thugs to break into our home at night, kick down the door and threaten to kill my family. Being pushed into my room, hidden away for my own safety did not stop the sounds, the banging, the screams. Then, it was all over. I was held tightly and felt a bubble of protection surround me, but not for long. My dad and brother were most at risk. The attackers seemed to hold back with the women and children because ironically even racists had bought into the patriarchal idea of females being the weaker gender. Authorities, neighbours and 'so called' friends turned their backs on us and we eventually ran out of choices.

Our beautiful home that I adored and held close to my heart was gone. We packed up, gave up the fight and made a move in order to save our lives. It still makes me sad that my parents walked away from everything they worked so hard to build. I yearn for the garden filled with apple trees and rhubarb that my mother would bake into my favourite apple crumble. I miss the wooden floors that were polished to perfection every weekend and which aided our childish games. Now, we could only afford to rent a mould filled home with the most depressing carpet I had ever seen. I commend the strength of my parents for holding it together in the face of such a terrible struggle.

What I've learned is that sometimes falling apart is the only route to rebuilding something new. We can use our intuition to make timely choices. Instead we procrastinate, agonise, close our eyes, refuse to budge and close the doorways to the natural flow of growth. When the resistance is too strong, life has a way of clearing the path for us. When we open ourselves up to change, we allow ourselves to grow and the gates open to flood in our favour.

After a turbulent time, my family pulled together and we bonded even more. Our unit itself, had always been firm but now seemed indestructible in my eyes. From the day I arrived, my parents demonstrated unconditional love and taught me to forgive. These lessons served me well when I faced relationship issues and chronic illnesses that forced me to go back to the basics.

I started a quest to seek knowledge from the world's best thinkers, healers and teachers. I put into practice what I had always known and now felt at the depths of my soul. I was able to understand that we all approach life from a different perspective. We all have our demons. We all want to fit in. Sometimes it's easier to hide amongst a crowd and conform even if that crowd are the furthest away from bringing out the best in us. I would like every reader to gift themselves with forgiving anyone or any situation that made them question their worth. This is not about agreeing with what occurred but releasing themselves from the impact because they deserve to be free.

When challenges come your way, you have a choice about how you will respond. You could freak out, bury your head in the sand, or, you could choose to transform it into something beautiful.

I never knew if I would ever reach this point, sharing and exposing my wounds openly. I believed I would be a weak person if I kept re-living and re-telling these stories, so I kept my voice hidden for many years. When it was found, so it was freed.

NADINE BARRETT

COACH, AUTHOR, PUBLIC SPEAKER

justmeonlife.com

Nadine Barrett is a coach, author and public speaker. She is the founder of "Just Me On Life Coaching" and supports men and women to find the lifestyle balance they need to play at 100% in their lives. She is a master at getting them to be clear about what they want, figuring out what's holding them back and teaching them to move forward with power and confidence.

In 2018 Nadine completed a 365-day Facebook live challenge and launched The Emerging Warrior Virtual Retreat. This was to show the world how commitment & alignment to your goals brings desired results. Above all, it was to prove that even an introvert can burst out of their comfort zone successfully.

"Brilliance is all around us. Learning to unleash it in others is the greatest gift we can provide to this world we live in."

- Sharon Bowes -

AFTER THE AVALANCHE

The pandemic toxic nature of the corporate world that impacts well meaning, hard working and even achiever driven employees negatively, can be such a spirit killer. Some would go as far as to take their own lives from the pressures of being laid off at work all the time. The familiar old feeling of being hit by an avalanche over and over again before you finally give up going in circles or climbing faster than anyone else to dodge it, makes you numb and eventually uncaring. Inevitably you stand within target range, hearing the rumble coming, completely expecting another hit and not being disappointed when it does happen, until…

That right there is the story of my life. I was that driven, well meaning employee who spent 20 years working diligently in 8 different organizations. I was convinced that I was probably the only employee in the world who defied the norm that if you worked well and achieved good things you were entitled to rewards and job security. I was so wrong. The harder I tried the more I became the victim of the layoff avalanche that was brought on by company changes, new ownership, global economic shifts or business closures.

Well, I will tell you that the first 3 layoff avalanches were the hardest to bounce back from and I felt left behind with a slowing career progress, living my days in fear, trying to prevent it from happening again. Then, I discovered that I could exploit the layoffs as a means to learning different skills faster. So, I stopped being anxious and welcomed the opportunity to move from workplace to workplace to learn new skills. Every time I got hit by an avalanche, I welcomed the opportunity to crack the new jackpot options and capitalize on an ever increasing salary. I deliberately chose my career objectives and growth path by lining up opportunities to learn faster, gaining a lot more experience in a much shorter timeframe than working with a single employer through this same series of years.

Fast forward - there were 4 more career layoffs, resulting in over 15 job transitions in a period of 15 years, I could see the next layoff coming, could hear the rumble of the releasing avalanche cornice, but I was now getting tired of the game. The avalanche hits were starting to get more painful, more difficult to climb out from under and I was feeling more and more frustrated. When I look back to that period of time, I realise that I was probably feeling that way because the time had come to do something better and that the universe was giving me a sign to prepare myself for it.

What happened next, changed everything.

My health took a turn for the worse as I started my new job and with hormonal replacement therapy at the same time, I started to have mood swings second to none. I continued to have dietary issues and I was fast becoming overweight and unhappy. Nothing was working the way I had planned and on the personal front my relationships were taking a beating too. My spirits hit a low and I reached rock bottom rapidly. I could no longer cope with the demands of the job and was forced to re-evaluate my choices. As my hormonal replacement therapy slowly but surely took effect, I started to experience positive mental and physical changes. I increasingly began to feel like I was meant to do something more and better with my life. I discovered that I was good at helping others and that I would be better off using my acquired skills to do something like this rather than trying to cope in corporate environments that sucked the life energy out of me daily, with the constant threat of that next avalanche to come.

What I had gained through it all, was an incredible set of skills in Management Consulting around Results and Transformation Management, heart-based coaching and influential partnership leadership. I could use this on a new career path! Of course, I first had to acknowledge that the path I had been on in the corporate world, was not one that was meant for me. I realized what I had known all along but had been afraid of accepting and that is that I am an entrepreneur and need to run my own business.

With a passion for lifelong learning and empowering the success of others, I established Going 4 Value Inc., a continuous development thought leadership community. I wrote "You're Not a Nail, the 7 Business Practices that Kill Innovation". I published this as an Interactive Seminar Series that has helped people increase their speed of learning and adopting new skills. Thought leaders are now enabled, empowered and supported by my team to publish their own Interactive Seminar Series to increase the speed of adoption for new thoughts and business practices.

I stepped out of the previous box I had put myself in and reached for greatness, and am here to help others do the same.

SHARON BOWES

CHANGE CATALYST AND ENTREPRENEUR

going4value.com

Beating all odds and capitalising on negative life altering experiences can be a very daunting way to live. Sharon Bowes did it over and over again in her career as she consciously made moves to grow and develop herself into the force to reckon with she is today.

Sharon specializes in coaching entrepreneurial thinkers by helping them to predictably achieve innovative, results. She uses insights from her new Interactive Seminar Series and Thought Leading Learning Community to create slingshot results generated from consciously directed energy that unleashes innovative thinking. She is a change catalyst and entrepreneur, understanding and leading with feminine power, harmoniously and with agile abilties second to none.

"You can do anything you decide because small daily actions will obtain staggering results."

- Naomi Carmona-Morshead -

GRANDMA ON A MISSION TO MEND 1000 HEARTS

The phone call came on a cold, wintery morning in January. The voice of a crying man said, "I'm sorry, honey, Mum went to heaven this morning." A sudden death, my 84-year-old father lost his wife of 65 years. For 21 days, our lives seemed worse than the winters that come to Southern California annually. We mourned the loss of a 'Godly' woman we all loved and admired.

With heavy hearts and Mum in our memories, my husband and I boarded a plane from Los Angeles to Quito, Ecuador. We had been adventure mountain climbers since 2015 and we were hiking the next 21 days up high-altitude glacier volcanoes planning to summit up to 20,564 feet (6,268 meters).

Here I was at 63 years old, an adult congenital open-heart surgery survivor of average health, a grandmother of seven beautiful grandchildren, risking my life to achieve a climb. Here I was with an ice axe in hand, crampons attached to my climbing boots, in freezing cold temperatures braving the odds of achieving a dream to be closer to my Mum in heaven. With the heavy snowfall I did not know if I was crazy. I didn't know if it was safe either but I did know that I was determined.

I had been living my life casually so as not to exacerbate my heart condition by engaging in extreme physical activities. As scared as I was of breaking the medical rules, it was at the "Circle of Champions" training, where I saw others younger than I was, do handstands, that I decided to throw away the banner that said "Never!" Suddenly the issues of my age, my heart, my breathing did not matter. I focused on new thought patterns: "I can do anything I decide to do." Shortly after starting my training, I did my first handstand for 33 seconds. I struggled for almost 4 days but with the encouragement from other students and all the cheering, I proved my persistence and extended my handstand personal record to 1 minute 31 seconds before I dropped to the ground crying and laughing at the same time. I broke through any anxieties I had and the emotional, spiritual and physical barriers vanished.

Following my wonderful husband's training regimen, I began hiking and climbing mountains in the USA, Mt. Kilimanjaro, Africa at 19,341 feet (5,900 meters) and finally, South America. Our expedition team was led by delightful, energetic Ecuadorans with six hikers from the USA. We first ascended two practice mountains and then climbed glacier-capped volcano Cayambe and Illiniza Norte with its "Death Step" climb.

Our final exciting snow-capped glacier climb was Chimborazo, the tallest volcanic mountain in the world when it is measured from the center of the earth 20,564 feet (6,263 meters). I was very excited to reach the summit which would bring me the closest to my Mum in heaven.

However, climbing would be no easy task. Dozens of cars were driving up the mountain from Quito filled with families and excited children wanting to play in the snow. The higher we drove the heavier the snow fell. The weather was not conducive for a safe climb. Our expedition leader explained that the snow on the upper mountain was thigh deep and the danger of an avalanche began at the elevation of 18,500 feet (5,638 meters). That wasn't very encouraging. We had high hopes, but our goal was looking dim. Of course, if the opportunity presented itself, we would stop at nothing to get to the top.

The guide did not even take our hiking boots out of the jeep. We sadly realized that the conditions would prevent us from climbing and we would not be able to achieve our goal. Depressed, I dressed in four layers of clothing anyway and walked out on the clouded mountain, right into the storm. The sunlight appeared, and I took it as a good sign.

My husband joined me and documented my final speech to my Mum on video. As I lay in the snow looking up, I could see her face smiling down from the clouds. As comforting as the vision was, I sobbed as I said my final goodbye. We left Quito with Mum engraved in my memory and soul forever.

Today, my husband and I are committed to a cause we call "Mending 1000 Hearts." Every day we make small strides conversing with people about helping children who have heart conditions who cannot afford heart surgery. We see them as the future of our nations and we want them to breathe properly again by mending their congenital heart structure issues and giving them hope and faith for better lives and futures. We are confident that though our consistent daily strides are small, the feeling of saving lives is sheer joy.

NAOMI CARMONA-MORSHEAD

INTERNATIONAL SPEAKER
AND MOUNTAIN CLIMBER

theBraveHeartShift.com

An international business woman and grandmother of seven, she has travelled to 49 states and 28 countries to become an Adventure Mountain Climber at the age of 61. Whether she is at ground zero or climbing altitude, she easily accomplishes both in the everyday business challenges of communication, technology and home life.

Whether she's navigating valleys or veering up steep mountains, over rocks and rock scrambles or being a participative family member, she is a force to reckon with and never backs down from a challenge. Whether she has her ice-climbing gear or her high-heeled shoes on, Naomi will tell you how Band-Aids have become a powerful boundary between pain and comfort. Readers will feel like they were on these outstanding adventures and become motivated to Climb Higher to reach the profound dreams of their youth.

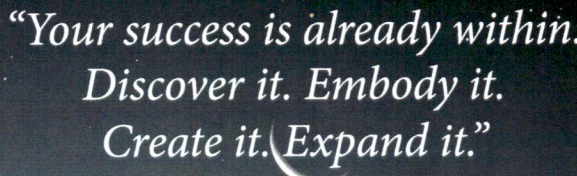

"Your success is already within.
Discover it. Embody it.
Create it. Expand it."

- Claire Chapman -

THE SUCCESS BOSS

I used to think of myself as just an ordinary mum and though everything must have looked perfect from the outside, I was depressed. What that meant was that on the inside I was silently unhappy and lived my life on auto mode. I had all the trimmings life could offer but that was of no use because I was depressed, bipolar and going through a painful divorce. Forlorn, bereft, abandoned and torn, I thought of every possible way to bring life to a close. I was on the edge, in a very deep dark place, at the point of no return. Yet would it make sense if I told you that somewhere deep down within there was also a struggle to live, to break through and to fight. It came from a burgeoning feeling that my depression had more to do with the need to be more and do more than a mere hormonal shift that caused me to be ill.

One day as I lay on the sofa in the living room, I physically froze. Although my body felt like it was paralysed, my eyes felt like they were seeing my children for the first time through a very different lens and I realised that I had to live, if not for me, then for them. Something very strange happened in that moment, something I had never felt before. It was as if I was on the outside looking in and if you have ever seen a slow motion, silent scene in a movie, then that is the perfect way to describe that moment in my life. Everything was quiet. The children, who were playing were silent as I watched them. Peace descended. Ease took over. My intuition found its voice and the voice said, "You need to help yourself." The words flashed before my eyes and my mind made its resolution.

I was on medication for the depression and bipolar disorder but that just provided balance for my mental state. I still had to work on a cure and the underlying problem. With the message still playing in my head, I put my children to bed and searched "Self Help" online. I found an incredible book called Love Life Live Life by Sue Stone and from that day onwards I have never looked back. I have grown and I have learnt so much about myself. I now understand the reason I had been attracting the negative into my life. With this knowledge, I have managed to turn the worst time in my life into an incredible blessing.

I stopped putting money into other people's pockets, I stopped shopping and I started to invest in myself. I spent my money wisely and went on amazing self-development programs, one of which was with Bob Proctor. You may have heard of him. He starred in the movie "The Secret." He taught me so much and showed me that I was born for bigger and better things. So, I knew I no longer wanted the regular, so called "Normal Life." I knew inside of me there was another way. I just had to find it and when I did, I came into my own and began to make the right kind of ripples in my life.

Most importantly, I am medication free, happy, healthy and on an absolute natural high. I am giving the best of myself to myself, my children and my newly founded business venture. I'm loving it!

During one of my meditation sessions, much like my original turning point on the sofa, another message came through to me. 'The Success Boss". I had no idea whether this was going to be a program for my business or a new company name but it made me feel good and it made me smile. The Success Boss revealed itself to be an embodiment of "Supreme Power". The Success Boss lives life working with the natural laws. The Success Boss turned into my personal success vision and partner to help me on my journey to achieving my life's goals.

I am finally free and I am living an "Unlimited Life" with purpose and success. It is not always easy and I of course, have moments in which I doubt myself and my journey. However, with the right people by my side and the right personal investments, my future has never looked brighter. I am never alone because my Success Boss always has my back. This is my belief system and it helps me to steer the course when doubt does kick in.

My biggest turning point and life achievement is being able to live my purpose and help others experience freedom, expansion and a successful way of living too.

This is exactly what I do and where I am today. I run my online company transforming the lives of others. It gives me the highest level of pleasure and satisfaction when I see my clients, training users and business partners succeeding, growing their level of awareness and most importantly, living the life they had previously only ever dreamed of.

The difference for them was making that decision, much as I did in that sofa moment, the decision that they were not happy with their current statuses and that they were going to reach out, invest and get the results they wanted.

No matter where you are in life, make that decision to change. If you don't change you will only get more of what you don't want. Remember you should always be evolving, always growing but never diminishing.

Think about it! Are you ready to make a difference? Are you ready to achieve those dreams and goals? Are you ready to meet your "Success Boss" and embody your own supreme power to live the life you desire?

CLAIRE CHAPMAN

THE SUCCESS BOSS

clairelouisechapman.com

After a tumultuous set of events, Claire has transformed her life in 2013 when she went from being a divorced, depressive and bipolar victim with two children to living a life of true success. On her journey, she discovered that success could not be found or bought. Instead it had to be created. Claire now utilises her personal experience to help others create and expand their own success. Although success is something very personal and unique, Claire believes there is so much more to us that is hidden deep within and with "The Success Boss" you can embody your own supreme power to live the life you desire.

"*Believe in yourself and in your power. There is no magic pill, magic mantra or magic wand. Life can be hard. Sometimes people are mean. Sometimes things don't go your way. You always have the power to CHOOSE and your choice should always consider your needs and dreams. You've got this!*"

- LaRissa Paras -

DOES FATE DRIVE YOU TO BECOME THE BEST VERSION OF YOURSELF?

Did fate get me to where I am today? Was it the tumultuous events of my life that led me to take action to change the course of it? Was it the wrong turns that I took that eventually brought me to the right place? Was it the relationship with my boyfriend that I was holding onto for too long that ironically brought me the man I am married to today? Those who are close to me and who know my journey intimately will agree, that it was and say exactly 'yes'. That is totally a valid opinion of what it looks like from the outside. I'm not regretful, or sad about that part of my life and rather grateful that it ended well and turned me into who I am today.

When I was in my teens, I stopped taking healthy risks. I did what was easy and safe for me to do. I chose a career that was solid, but not my dream. I had a long-term boyfriend and used him as an excuse to keep me from reaching out for my dreams of travel and pursuing an exploratory career. I wasn't the most athletic, so I decided to stop exercising. I started to feel like I had to stop expressing my opinions because it was just safer to be quiet. I stopped asking questions so I wouldn't appear to be stupid and eventually started hating my body enough to develop an eating disorder.

I rapidly lost touch with who I really was and though others were happy to have me that way, I often felt like I was trapped in a body that could never live up to the expectations I saw in my head or in a glossy magazine. I felt the pressure for perfection to the point where I felt frozen in my own life.

Often, the overwhelming need to say "no" to what I didn't really want washed over me, however I remained speechless, unable to communicate my own needs and preferences to the people in my life. Too often, the words would come to the top of my throat, my tongue readying itself to utter the words that would probably have freed me, yet the words would get quashed and I'd swallow them. The all too "familiar ball of hurtful desperation" would find it's way back down my gut, the welling tears would get pushed to the back of my eyes and I'd smile again and agree to things I didn't really want. I was a people pleaser and it was destroying my life, my identity and my self-confidence.

However, there was a voice deep inside me somewhere also that kept telling me to break free, voice my feelings and do the things I wanted to do. I started to take more notice of how other women were conducting their careers, personal lives and relationships and I started to secretly aspire to better things for myself. When the aspirations got strong enough, I realised that I needed to work on myself first and that was when I tried yoga as a means to the end.

It was my introduction to yoga that got me in touch with my breath, my mind, and my body. It gave me a place to find clarity and calm, a place to just be in my own head and to think my very thoughts and connect with my body in a positive way. Some people like jogging, kneeling in prayer, or walking in the woods. However, yoga gave me back my self-esteem, as I felt my body grow strong again. When I look back on that time of my life and try to find out what made me take it up, I realise that somewhere I just made a choice one day to stop being miserable. I realise that when I made that conscious choice, my life changed forever and definitely for the better. "Make a conscious choice," has since become my mantra for living this beautiful gift we call life.

I also discovered that looking within and finding clarity can be uncomfortable because you could be forced to deal with pent up emotions that you have kept suppressed. I have broken down crying in the middle of a yoga class before. It felt like my body couldn't hold in the anxiety I was feeling any longer. But it also felt good to let it go and I am since more open to this kind of clarity and emotions during yoga.

I also started surrounding myself with people that made me a better person. Did I find them or did they find me? Were we all energies seeking each other or was it just kismet? I don't know for sure. What I do know, is that these people were supportive, encouraging and wise. They challenged me in the healthiest of ways. They corrected me when I said something derogatory about myself and didn't realise it. They loved me unconditionally and showed me a better way of dealing with all facets of my life. It was among them, that I re-learned to voice my opinions, apply my mind and communicate in ways I never thought possible. They showed me that it's okay to be vulnerable, but also how to be strong and overcome it.

I am now more of a "in control of my own destiny" kind of girl. I think our choices, good or bad, lead us to where we are in life. Our decisions create these events, lead to eye-opening experiences, the life partner, the career, and the relationships we share with people we meet and invite into our lives.

We can jump at the opportunities that come our way or we can choose to ignore them. This is not to say that everything goes according to our plans. If the first thing we try doesn't work, we have the option to keep trying or to give up. It took me a long time to realise that fate wasn't making all of my decisions for me, but I was making them for myself. It is my mission to help young people learn this skill earlier than I did myself.

LARISSA PARAS

PUBLIC SPEAKER, MENTOR, FOUNDER OF THE LOTUS PROJECT

lpinspire.com

LaRissa is an alumna of Central Michigan University and State University of New York. A tenured teacher, she previously worked in New York and then in Michigan, where she now resides with her loving husband and two beautiful sons.

A co-author on the high school US History textbook for the Michigan Open Books Project, she is a also a youth mental health first aid practitioner. LaRissa is a yoga instructor and a Cognitive Coach as well. She founded the Lotus Project which is a mentoring program curriculum that is designed to help adults mentor teen girls and give them the tools they need to succeed. She enjoys public speaking and therefore leads workshops on important subjects like Mentoring, Positive Self Talk, Manifesting and Maintaining Healthy Relationships.

"A woman's worst day in the United States is infinitely better than a woman's best day in many parts of the world. It's imperative that those of us with more in our lives, take action on behalf of those with less."

- Debra Dion Krischke -

INSPIRED WOMEN
PAYING IT FORWARD

While the seed of my core values of giving back were planted early in my life, it took root and germinated when I was fresh out of college and had the opportunity to join my parents in Iran as a travel coordinator with Grumman's F-14 program. Whilst there, I noticed a little girl under a full chador attempting to play on a seesaw on a playground. It was wrong on so many levels, but little did I know that assisting "Fearless Women under Veil" would be a lifelong commitment for me. Seeing women under veil and the oppression they had to deal with on a daily basis were defining images for me. I knew I had to advocate for women and girls who didn't have a voice.

The road leading to "Inspired Women Paying it Forward" was often full of bumps and even huge boulders, so tripping, stumbling and even falling was something that happened frequently. I always share these struggles openly to inspire other women on their personal journeys. I lived in Iran just before the revolution, unaware that global women's education would become my passion. I've been a women's advocate my entire adult life and a tireless fundraiser for women's initiatives such as domestic violence, trafficking, and global girl's education.

On September 11th, 2001, when the world was reeling from the attacks on the US, my personal world was in turmoil too. The title sponsors of my 5-Day Paintball Festival, with whom I had enjoyed a 10-year relationship, called to say that they were backing out of our contract. Complicating matters was the fact that my entrepreneurial husband, Ryan's business in Information Technology, was in jeopardy since the implosion of the Dot com industry six months prior. Our income was precarious, and now this horrific tragedy would surely affect our nation's economic stability and sense of safety for years to come.

However, I continued to delve into every conceivable idea to help women. Formerly as a restaurateur, I hired as many single mothers as possible. Later I produced a foodie fundraiser in our home and then turned this event into a business model. I took it on the road and worked with selected groups of women. This helped them gain needed visibility in the market place, assisting them to earn upwards of $20,000.

This is when I hit another obstacle in the form of naysayers. Questions were raised as to why I trademarked it and why I wasn't doing this as a volunteer, or perhaps I was only interested in my own financial gain. Like a pillow torn open, rumors and gossip soon spread like feathers creating doubt around the very values I always believed in.

Betrayal taught me how to move past it and at the same time equipped me to help others overcome similar setbacks. It showed me that all women in leadership positions went through this and I wasn't the only one. I started working with a corporate trainer who gave me the tools I didn't have. Her wisdom, skillset and expertise became a lifeline for me. As a student, I was ready and when I was ready, the teacher appeared. Once again, I was affirmed as a believer in faith, destiny, the power of the universe and setting intentions.

Established in 2015 in Pittsburgh, Pennsylvania, "Inspired Women Paying it Forward" now has 3 chapters in our city and we have raised over $110,000 for women's non-profits and agencies that do the heavy lifting for women in need. This is a model for philanthropic networking, one hour, once a quarter, raising up to

$10,000 per quarter on behalf of women's non-profits locally and globally. And this is just the beginning.

Our vision is to assist opening chapters worldwide. Members are able to vote and to nominate with a commitment of just $100 a quarter going to the winning charity. It's collective giving with a collective impact.

There are countless women across the globe whose core values include helping other women and paying it forward. Each quarter, many such women approach our chapters to honor their desire. We make opportunities available for constituents who are in a position to launch a chapter in their areas. Participants get the opportunity to honor their values and also get the chance to showcase their businesses while connecting with others interested in collaborating. This is not a means to earn money personally, but it definitely provides participants with the visibility and networking opportunities that every business needs to succeed.

What makes this opportunity even more attractive is the option for participants to nominate any women's non-profit they may feel passionately about. They can also learn about the amazing agencies and NGOs that work on behalf of women issues. All of this takes just one hour, once a quarter making it fast, efficient and soul-filling.

A friend of mine and founder of the non-profit "SowHope" recently shared what she learned from "the Wisest Man in Pakistan", a man who consented to seeing her only because of her global efforts on behalf of women. She asked him, "Why are women treated so badly in so many parts of the world?" After thinking for a moment, he smiled and responded, "Women have all the power, they just don't believe it yet."

Inspired Women Paying it Forward is proof of this. Recently our Pittsburgh chapters collectively donated over $12,000 to Sister Zeph's school in Pakistan. Despite the long, bumpy road, I have finally created a sustainable business model to raise significant funds for women across the globe who need our assistance now more than ever.

DEBRA DION KRISCHKE

INSPIRED WOMEN PAYING IT FORWARD

InspiredWomen.com

Debra Dion Krischke is a passionate women's advocate and special event producer. Her company Team Effort Events has raised over 2 million dollars and brought much needed awareness to women's initiatives locally and globally. In 2015 she launched "Inspired Women Paying it Forward," a quarterly, philanthropic networking group.

A recipient of numerous awards, in 2006, Debra was honored as one of Governor Rendell's "50 Best Women in Business". She co-authored "Inspired Entrepreneurs – A Collection of Female Triumphs in Business and Life" and remains committed to helping women to be as successful as possible, no matter what stage of life they are at, so that they are in a better position to Pay it Forward!

"It's not what happens to you, but how you choose to live every single day, which defines you."

- Victoria Drake -

FALL DOWN 7 TIMES, GET UP 8

I'm a Holistic Success Coach from the North West of England. My greatest dream is to help thousands of women achieve and exceed their wildest dreams by creating successful businesses that make the world a better place, while creating a life they love. I had no idea this would be my path in life but it all started when I was still a third year university student, finishing my Policing Degree and working as a Special Constable in my spare time. On the night in question I was on my first ever response and night shift…

I was shivering despite my jacket as we banged on the door of a grimy block of flats for the fourth time. It was three in the morning and we'd received a call of a domestic incident from a neighbour. Four of us arrived at the scene, but so far, all attempts to enter the block were futile. We were just turning away when a woman, white in the face, hurtled down the stairs, fumbling to open the door. "Help him, help him, he's not breathing!" She gasped. We bolted up the stairs, taking two at a time. Booting open the door we were confronted with a man, motionless on the floor, his face ashen.

As my partner performed CPR, I scanned the flat for clues as to what had happened finding, to my horror, a pile of needles in the bathroom. Making a swift retreat I noticed my partner flagging.

"Here, let me." Switching places with him and placing my hands over the man's heart, I put everything into saving his life. I failed.

En route to retrieving the scene tape from the car I disposed of my gloves in the ambulance which had arrived, barely thinking to glance at them. Then I looked at my hands; they were somehow bloody, and with broken skin from eczema, I had just potentially contracted a blood borne virus.

It's funny how being face to face with death puts life into perspective. That and the looming possibility of having a life-threatening illness. For what felt like an age I huddled in my room, dry heaving from the antiretroviral medication I'd been given as a precaution, feeling like I'd been hit by a train. I was depressed.

Then one day, as I sat in bed, I was suddenly enveloped in a profound sense of calm. In my mind's eye I saw a vision of myself in bed, before the image zoomed far out, above my flat, above the world and out into space and time, until I saw the present earth on a line of earth's past and future, stretching as far as the eye could see in all directions. I realised then just how tiny I was, utterly miniscule, in the grand scheme of things. But whilst I only occupied a fraction of the earth's space and time, I occupied all of mine. Nobody else would ever get to be me. In a world of infinite possibility, I was free to do as I pleased, no one else cared and that was great!

I thought that if I could spring into action to try save a man's life, I could surely be the hero of my own story? I resolved to write the next chapter every day, for the rest of my life. I was the author now and I was excited that I got to choose which direction the story would go.

The next day I signed up to an MMA class and began bodybuilding. I began researching how to build the house of my dreams, researched mindset day and night and placed my application for the job of my dreams as an investigator with the English FBI.

I got into the shape of my life, I walked around with my head held high, if I saw a cute guy at the bar, I'd walk up to him and say 'hi', I improved my mindset every single day and I got the job. Oh, and my blood tests came back negative. Big sigh of relief.

I've been on a whistle-stop journey since then, everything from depression to break ups and weight fluctuations have tried to stop me from moving forward, but I haven't forgotten that I'm a survivor and I am always in control of what happens on the next page of my story.

An unexpected relationship breakdown left me suddenly homeless in the middle of the night. With my family living on the other side of the country, I had nowhere to go. I had just left my job and had no way of supporting myself either. My world fell apart again, but this time I was resourceful and braver and though things were difficult initially, I slowly recovered. I reminded myself to pick up my pen again and write the next pages of my story. I had all the tools I needed to succeed. With the business skills I'd acquired from a previous job, I set out to help women change the world through entrepreneurship, and I haven't looked back since.

A year and a half later I'm a homeowner, I have a loving partner and I've helped so many women achieve their dreams that it makes my head spin. From the homebased salon product creator who reached her income goal in two months of working with me, to the autistic woman who is making waves in a full time job for the first time in 20 years and fully focused on starting her own business to spread awareness around autism; I have been privileged for my story to have been shared with people across the globe, and I hope it helped you too. Go write your story, Warrior, pick up your pen.

VICTORIA DRAKE

HOLISTIC SUCCESS COACH

becomeawarrior.co.uk

Victoria is a holistic success coach whose mission in life is to help women with world changing business ideas and transform them into reality whilst creating a life that they love. From an unconventional background, Victoria leads her warrior tribe to success and freedom.

Her own experiences are the foundation from which she drives her business and ensures that others too, are given the tools they need to overcome, to excel and to supersede their own expectations of themselves. Victoria leads others from the heart and has an uncanny ability to read her clients accurately through sharp intuition. These natural abilities are the reason for her astounding success.

"Your business and life do not get better by chance. They get better through change. Moving forward with imperfection and taking responsibility for your own destiny is your guaranteed path to growth and expansion."

- Vicky Etherington -

YOUR DREAMS ARE WITHIN YOUR REACH

Being born with a veil over your face occurs in fewer than one in eighty thousand births and is often thought to signify a special destiny, psychic abilities and good luck. I was born at home, with a veil over my face on a sunny June morning, just as my brothers were leaving for Sunday school. I don't hold any psychic abilities, and I'm not sure of any special destiny yet, but I do know that I have been blessed with unusual luck.

My story isn't one of hardship and despair - it's one of an ordinary life that became remarkable through happenstance and adventure.

Freedom and adventure were always an integral part of my life.

Having travelled around Europe and Central America with friends from school and university, I saved enough money after my first real job to set off for Fiji with a round-the-world ticket in my pocket.

Several years later, I still hadn't returned home. I worked whenever I ran out of cash, lived on a shoestring budget and loved every minute of it. It was a charmed existence, full of extraordinary encounters and remarkable experiences.

After several years, I found myself living in a small wooden hut on the edge of the most crocodile and hippo infested river in

Africa, in a remote corner of Zambia. I could not have felt more at home. Every day brought a new adrenaline rush adventure with wildlife more abundant than in my craziest dreams, and inspired by my experiences there, I became actively involved in African conservation projects.

It was in 2003 that I eventually returned to the UK and I was married the following year. I married someone in the British army, without having any kind of appreciation of what that would involve. Within 3 months of being married, we were heading out to Germany for our first married posting. It was where we had first met 10 years previously, and where I had studied at University, and so it felt like a happy coincidence to start our life together there.

A few months later, my new husband was posted to Iraq for 5 months, and I found myself home alone. Shortly into his tour, he called me in great excitement about a trip he was taking from Basra to Baghdad where he would have an opportunity to see one of our dear friends who was based there with the US military.

His parting words were that I wasn't to worry, as he would be flying there by helicopter and it was the safest way to travel.

The following morning, I heard reports of a British army helicopter being shot down in Basra. Everyone on board had been killed. It had been on its way to Baghdad. The three days of silence, which followed were torturous and no one had any answers for us.

The first time I knew my husband was still alive, was when he called me three days after the incident, and my happiness to hear from him was quickly overshadowed by the guilt that my relief was someone else's grief. It was a brutal eye-opener to the world of the military.

In the 11 years that followed, my husband was away for about 5 of them, either on operational tours in Iraq, Afghanistan and Libya, or on exercises, preparing for his next overseas tour. And within those 11 years, we moved house 10 times. Packing boxes and unpacking boxes became something of a regular pastime for me.

Starting my own business amid this kind of upheaval was testing. Building any kind of team around me, or putting roots down was impossible. The 'gig culture' hadn't started yet, and so I fell into a routine of doing everything in the business by myself.

In truth, I didn't fully appreciate the demands of running my own business, and I certainly wasn't valuing my own time.

10 weeks after our second child was born, my husband left at 2 hours' notice to go away, allegedly for one week. 5 months later, he still hadn't returned. The operation he was on was shrouded in secrecy, and we had no idea of when he would return. Our new baby suffered from silent reflux, which meant that as an infant, he barely slept.

It was around the same time that I was diagnosed with an excruciating condition called 'trigeminal neuralgia' and it opened my eyes to the fact that things had to change. It took 10 years of entrepreneurship and a medical crisis for me to realise that I was burning out. I had more clients than I could deal with, was working crazy hours, had hit my income ceiling and was trading time for money. I invested in a mentor and started turning things around.

For the first time, I started putting boundaries around the projects that I would accept, and recognised the value I was delivering to my clients.

Building confidence in the services I was offering, enabled me to stop trading hours for dollars. I switched my business model from done-for-you services, to training coaches how to build their own websites, and in doing so, I was able to work with so many more people and have since helped hundreds of entrepreneurs take control of their own online marketing.

If only I had had the courage to invest in myself sooner, step out of my comfort zone and surround myself with a network of like-minded entrepreneurs, I would be 10 years ahead of where I am today. But it was all part of the journey.

VICKY ETHERINGTON

THE WEBSITE MENTOR

thewebsitementor.com

A pioneer in the digital world, Vicky set up her online marketing agency in 2003. She teaches coaches and therapists how to create their own client-attracting websites, rise above the noise, thrive at entrepreneurship, master technology with confidence and stay on track.

With a bigger vision of working with entrepreneurial women in the rural areas of Africa to help communities break the cycle of poverty, Vicky is passionate about helping entrepreneurs closer to home as well, and loves to see coaches, therapists and change-makers conquer their fears, drive their businesses forwards with confidence and realise their dreams.

"No one can save you from yourself but you. No one can walk your walk but you. No one can shield you from your storms better than you. But whether you're saving, walking or shielding, you will find the brightest rainbows at the end of them all."

- Louise Green -

FROM TRAGEDY TO DISCOVERING MY TRUE LIFE PURPOSE

Up until the age of 36 my life had been relatively easy. I had a happy childhood, did well at school and studied for a degree in Maths. I was never sure about what I wanted to do as a career, so I fell into Merchandising. I was good at my job and it gave me enough money to travel the world, however I knew deep down it wasn't my true passion. I knew that I didn't want to do it forever and it was a tragic series of events that led me to discover my life's purpose.

It was May 2010 and I was pregnant. My husband and I were both surprised and delighted to discover at our first scan that we were expecting twins. We told our families our exciting news and then learnt that twins were our family heritage. My Mum told me that my great grandmother sadly had stillborn twins. I remember thinking that it was okay and there was nothing to worry about. It was a long time ago and medicine had moved on since then. Nothing was going to dampen our excitement.

A few months later I found myself in hospital with pre-eclampsia. As my health deteriorated, the consultant advised us to deliver the boys early. We agreed and the date was set and planned for. Then the day before they were due to be born, my whole world was turned upside-down. Through routine monitoring of my babies, only a single heartbeat could be detected. I was rushed to have an urgent scan and was told the devastating news that my son James had died. I was in shock, had an emergency C section and my surviving son, Thomas, was taken straight to intensive care. As he was born at 34 weeks, he was unable to breathe or feed independently. That first night after they were born, I spent alone with my husband, without a baby, devastated, trying to absorb what had just happened, nothing making sense, nothing soothing my pain, nothing healing the ache in my heart. If anybody would have told me that feeling a literal ache in the heart was possible, I'd never have believed it till that night.

Two weeks later both my survivor and I were well enough to leave the hospital and return home and we discovered that there was an undiagnosed medical condition in my family that was the cause of James' death. At the time I wanted to hide, protect my son and not have him live with the label 'The surviving twin.' It was my amazing pregnancy yoga teacher who supported me to leave the house and start attending classes with other mums. I found it so difficult to deal with the mixed emotions I was feeling, as well as coping with others reactions to what had happened. Fortunately I had her support and I coped.

2 years later my rainbow baby Emily was born. I was elated to have a baby to bring home from hospital. However, when she was a month old she had her own medical drama when she developed bronchiolitis and had to be blue lighted into hospital. She thankfully recovered but it resurrected all the old feelings I had when the boys were born. I remember asking myself why all my children faced dire situations. I blamed myself and labelled myself a bad mother. Deep down I knew this wasn't true but I sought a holistic therapist to support and help me deal with my PTSD. As I am a spiritual yogi who loves Reiki and other energy work, so I wanted to take a holistic approach to my healing. After all, my children needed their mother.

Through my counselling sessions she taught me how to deal with the difficult situations life threw at me and helped me heal from the trauma. She showed me how I could build a life after loss without feeling guilty. It took time and I was able to create a new life and a new 'normal'. A year later I felt guided to work through a transformational life coaching program which allowed me to further heal from my grief.

I am so grateful to both these women for working with me and I know nothing I can do in return could ever repay them. I desperately wanted to do something special for them and the opportunity came a few years later at a Cacao ceremony where I connected with my higher self and helped one of them to thrive in their business. My own business was born. I was honoured that one of the women who supported me became my first client.

I now work solely with heart-centred entrepreneurs because I know how important the work they do is and how they can make a massive positive impact in the world. It's my mission to help these businesses succeed and it is my way of paying back in gratitude. I have now discovered my life's purpose and I feel blessed that it was my son James that was the catalyst to me finding my calling.

LOUISE GREEN

ONLINE BUSINESS MANAGER

louisejgreen.com

Louise Green is an online business manager who works with established heart-centered entrepreneurs looking to grow and upscale their businesses. She shows them how to put profit systems into their businesses and helps them take it to the next level.

As a spiritual yogi, with a love of numbers, she applies her 14 years' experience of working in corporate retail, to help her clients to turn wellness into wealth. By using her complementary skills, she enables people to focus on what they do best.

Her mission is to pay it forward to the holistic community that supported her through PTSD following the stillbirth of her son James.

"Where there is a will for happiness there is a way to get there. All you have to do is follow your instinct."

- Kusha Kalra -

I AM LOVE &
I GROW DAILY

I am definitely not defined by my past experiences and I am very sure that they shaped and prepared me for the life I lead today. Three major challenges occurred during my lifetime and each one of them taught me different lessons that I am eager to share in this story. Hi, I'm Kusha Kalra, owner of The Bespoke Designs. I wear many hats and am a woman of many shades and talents. Today, I help people overcome their struggles of converting words to visuals using graphic designs to exhibit class, sass and razzmatazz in their businesses. I had never worn so many hats with such confidence, but what else would you expect from a rebellious, ultra-positive, bold, blunt, kind, sweet with 'a dash of salt personality'? I can't help it. I was born to be fabulous.

Life was just gorgeous until I married a man who was abusive. Divorce in the community I come from is somewhat taboo and one of the biggest challenges any woman faces. I tried to make it work like every woman does for a long time but once my loving and adorable son was born, I realised that I could not allow him to be raised in a toxic environment. Fathers set a major example for the way future generations treat the women in their circles and my husband was not going to set a proper one for my son.

So, I gathered my wits and strength and as tough as it was, I walked away when my son was just 4 months old. It's been eight years since I did that and I'm grateful for the freedom I have to raise my son in a peaceful, stimulating and secure environment. This experience taught me what it means to be strong and confident in the face of grave danger. It also taught me that my intuition is my friend, that if I listened it to and acted upon it, I'd be the happier with my choices.

The one thing that I was excelling at was my job. As a facilitator, I was responsible for shaping the lives and futures of thousands of students that I trained over the years. It was a matter of pride and joy for me once I became a mother it also became my greatest challenge. It isn't always easy to balance being a single mum with the expectations that come with being a high-flyer in the corporate training environment. Long training hours, planning courses and additional responsibilities that you sometimes don't sign up for, become the order of the day. Whilst I enjoyed my job I also desperately wanted to be there for my son and that wasn't happening on a full time, action packed schedule.

I was introduced to coaching and a whole new world about myself opened up for me. I started to research the possibilities of becoming a coach, as I truly felt that if I pursued it and started to work for myself, I'd be able to give both my son and myself a better quality of life. So, I attended seminars, programmes and started to develop my skills and talents in the area of coaching as well. It was my crush and I enjoyed every bit of change and growth I was experiencing.

At around this point in time, it also came to light that my business partner betrayed me. In stark contrast to the partnership agreement we had, it was I who was left with all the work whilst he profited from it. I instinctively knew that the time had come for me to pursue the online business world and though there were so many risks involved, I ditched the dead beat partnership and took the plunge.

I worked at manic speed to make my online business a reality. I stopped taking on new coaching clients and focused on honing my sales and marketing skills. I hired coaches, bought online courses and tried to cover every possible aspect I'd need to make a success of myself. The Bespoke Designs took off, although I have had many challenges along the way and many lessons to learn. I can happily admit that the decision I made to become an entrepreneur was the best decision of my life. From all the lessons I have had to learn so far - the one that stands out the most is, "Open your shop daily."

What that basically means is that when you are running your business from behind a computer screen every day, it is vital that you are visible both to your current and future clients all the time. Whether that's in the form of advertising, posting photographs or doing live videos, you have to do different things every day to catch and hold attention.

I had many challenges learning to do online videos. I overcame my fears by accepting live Facebook challenges in different groups and I discovered that the more I did it, the better I became at it. I know I have a long way to go to perfection and I am glad that I have made my first breakthroughs.

My experiences in life and business have taught me that you should choose who you invite into your life and financial circle very carefully. Take nothing for granted and ensure that your inner circles are trustworthy and honourable. Trust your intuition wholly and go after what you seek with all your heart. Love what you do and don't ever doubt yourself.

KUSHA KALRA

DESIGNYLIST

thebespokedesigns.com

Kusha Kalra is known to herself as a Designylist, which means that she is a design and style coach for women entrepreneurs online. She is also a certified Life Coach and trainer with extensive experience in the corporate environment for 15 years. Her passion is women in leadership and development and she specialises in helping them improve their lives, overcome guilt, shame and embarrassment.

She helps women make quantum success in business by taking small, actionable steps to build their brands. She is a passionate, visionary and specialises in helping online entrepreneurs with finding creative solutions through design and style for their businesses.

"Yes, sometimes it won't be an easy ride, and of course your path will have ups and downs. However, believe that your success is inevitable and it will be because YOU are a gorgeous wonder-woman – ready to thrive, shine, and matter."

- Konnie Labecki -

THE WATCHWORD
IS DECLUTTER

I want you to picture a woman, tired and mentally frazzled, two children to raise and completely out of sync with life. She's trying to be everything that she thinks she has to be for everyone but herself. She's mentally, emotionally and physically depleted, crying on the sofa is her regular pastime and numbing pain in a discontent lifestyle is a regular feature.

This was me, Konnie Labecki, right up until June 2017. Until that point, I'd had enough, snapped and decided that radical change was in order. I took the first step, called my husband, discussed my plan and began my journey into a life I envisioned and yearned for.

Discovering an NLP programme was a happy accident. Since I had my husband's support, I jumped on a plane with my nanny and two children and went to London. It was the best massive action I could ever have taken in my life. I simply enjoyed the process, made lifelong friends and committed to doing whatever it took. I was ready to release all my limiting self beliefs and take responsibility for my life. I didn't have a definite plan by the end of it but I did leave with a clearer vision of my ideal life.

My intuition guided me to healing and recovery from the fatigue I was feeling, so I went to San Francisco on an unplanned break. With my kids in tow, I simply relaxed and let the training I had just completed seep into my conscience. It was the best move because soon after the break I began journaling. Although it is a very understated tool, it is my belief that journaling about things that I was grateful for, all manifested themselves into my life. I journaled about everything from my ideal business and personal life, my life's mantras to my own affirmations and visionary statements. It also helped to replace the negative, self limiting mind chatter and SOS conferences I used to house as my thoughts. I now had feelings of acceptance, thoughts of a better future and anticipated feelings of abundance. I was sure that an ideal lifestyle was around the corner. These moments of self awareness were a game-changer for me so much so that I decided to become an NLP coach. The definite plan had come and I began my journey into my awesome profession.

The next thing I did was start building my spiritual side. I intuitively felt, I needed to connect with God and this helped me have faith that the road I was on was the correct one. It helped build self belief and my negative internal talk became a thing of the past. I stopped having friends who did not support me, were jealous of me or who were negative all the time. I simply did not have space for that in my life and though this was a positive step, it did dredge up memories of being bullied in my past. Suddenly, the possibilities of being lonely scared me again.

Thanks to the NLP training, I realised the importance of minimizing the presence of people who were not 'in my corner'. I even decluttered unnecessary things in the house and I continue to do it even today. The process of decluttering took my business from 0 to multiple 4-digit figures in a short space of time. Decluttering regularly brings me the kind of clarity I need to take my life to the next level all the time. I am also convinced that removing things you don't need makes place for things you really want.

I also realised that with decluttering comes the process of forgiveness and so I started a 'Forgiveness list' to which I have added the names of people who have hurt me or who I have hurt and I continue to add to this list even now. The simple practice of writing words like, 'I forgive you,' 'I'm sorry,' 'I love you,' are simple ways of putting negative relationships behind you and moving on.

I have also started a list of everything that I want to Be, Do and Have. This list evolves and grows and I'm fine with that because it gives me something to work towards all the time. I read it and add to it daily and call this my 'Power-hour.'

Being a coach, I also recognise the importance of being coachable. I therefore have a personal coach who works with me on those areas of my life, in which I need to build myself. I know that this is working for me, because through it I give myself the permission to live my desires, know my strengths intimately, go after my goals passionately and prioritise my life a little selfishly and protectively.

Here's what I know about life now and feel so excited to add value to yours by sharing it. Decluttering and forgiveness are the main things that you need to do to make space for a bigger and better life. Your core values are the things you need to take with you wherever you go and everything you do should be aligned to that. Otherwise, you're likely to be less inclined to commit to it. You need to be clear and precise about what it is you want in your life otherwise you will end up with a fraction of what you really want. Support what you want with a positive heart and mind and have faith that God will help you get what you really want. Be inspired by your goals and take massive action to make them happen, otherwise they will remain just dreams. You are the only 'V.I.P' in your life and nothing and no one is more important than you and your vision for a fulfilling life.

KONNIE LABECKI

SPEAKER AND AUTHOR, FOUNDER OF SIMPLY ORGANIZED

simplyorganizedwithkonnie.com

Konnie Labecki is CEO and founder of Simply Organized with Konnie. A speaker and author, she holds certifications as an NLP Coach (American Board of Neuro Linguistic Programming) and Professional Organizer (National Association of Productivity & Organizing Professionals) with training from the American Board of Hypnosis.

Konnie provides training, coaching and consulting to individuals and small business owners where her mission is to motivate and inspire professionals to uncover and develop their strengths through releasing what holds them back, like limiting beliefs and physical, emotional and mental clutter.
She helps people to create space for truth, clarity, passions, and the ability to thrive and live a First Class Life – physically, mentally and emotionally.

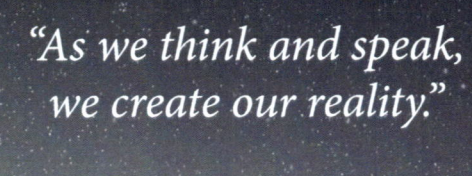

"As we think and speak,
we create our reality."

- Felicia Lonobile -

IT'S ALL IN THE STATE OF MIND

My name is Felicia, and I admit that I have lived most of my adult life denying myself a chance at a good, wholesome life because I lacked self-esteem and let fear, doubts, and insecurities run every aspect of my life. I was confused, lost and in search of a life purpose. I blamed everyone else for my problems and often felt unappreciated. To my mind, everyone but myself, was responsible for my pain. I was the champion of self-sabotage and everything that went wrong with what I did, happened because I never paid a single positive thought or gave a single atom of positive energy to anything I did.

Living this kind of life caused me a lot of pain. The more I hurt myself the more resentful I was becoming of my situation, the deeper I was sinking. It was so out of control that although I warned myself over and over again to stop the self-destruction, I could not stop myself. I hoped repeatedly that someone would see that I needed help and love and come to my rescue because that was the state of my mind. That didn't happen because in time the pain became increasingly unbearable, consuming, and disturbing. I knew I could no longer ignore the signs and one morning I reached deep within and resolved to stop my destructive behavior in its tracks.

In those moments of initial decision-making, I was still in a terrible place of darkness, fighting relentlessly to break through the feelings of emptiness and confusion. Then, in a few moments of clarity, I experienced what pain, shame and self-destructive thoughts I had brought on myself. At the same time, I buried my old story, the false one, and embraced a new purpose, a new way of thinking, a new way of behaving and a new way of taking on life. A new Felicia was born, and she was here to stay. I liked her! I just had to figure out what she wanted to do and be.

It didn't take long for me to discover what I wanted to do and when it did come, I experienced magic. It was like a revelation. I got an inspiring thought, and I decided to trust my intuition. It paid off in ways I never imagined would be possible. In those moments, I remember feeling more joy and bliss than I ever have my whole life and I suddenly knew that everything was going to be fabulous. To have these moments of self-discovery, I simply took a moment to ask myself what I would absolutely love doing, and I decided to do just that.

I was ready for a change, and although I didn't know what I was going to do exactly to get to my dream life, I saw myself make conscious decisions to do things differently. Every time I found myself having one of those old, useless and self-destructive thoughts, I broke the pattern by ignoring it and replaced it with positive self-talk and actions. I filled my life with joy and laughter and left no place for fear, anxiety or doubt. I knew I was far greater than any situation or circumstance I was facing. Merely shifting my perception by one degree changed my life in ways I never even thought possible.

Opportunities that would not otherwise show up began falling into my lap. I started to manifest people, places and things that would prepare me for the life I was meant to lead. I was open to learning, and teaching and the more I got to learn, the more I got to teach. In teaching, I was serving, and in serving, I was being rewarded because nothing came second to the emotions I felt when I was doing this. The old Buddhist proverb that when the student is ready, the teacher will appear, rang true and then, there was no looking back. I enrolled to become a transformational life coach and a certified Life Mastery consultant.

During the time I spent learning, I discovered the opportunity to help people through speaking, teaching, coaching and mentoring. If you have ever been fortunate enough to feel your calling, you would know what I was feeling and you would know that I was flying through the process of becoming the best version of myself. I'll never deny that I was scared at times and that I never really knew how it would all work out. I leaped in and learned to fly on the journey into the unknown.

Today, I'm living the dream. I wake up each day impassioned for the life I love. I wake up with the feeling of loving my life. I would not be where I am today if it were not for that fateful but victorious morning in which, I decided to listen to the small voice of intuition and take action on it. We are far more than the physical bodies that we are. We are spiritual beings having a human experience, and if we thought about life more this way, we would stop punishing ourselves the way we do and start living the way we should. Our purpose in life is for no other reason than to live happily ever after, and as children of God, it's our birthright to live the life we love.

FELICIA LONOBILE

LIFE MASTERY CONSULTANT
AND RESULTS EXPERT

felicialonobile.com

As a Certified Life Mastery Consultant and Results Expert, Felicia can help you design and manifest a life that's in harmony with your soul's purpose.

For over 10 years, Felicia has been studying and implementing transformational success principles, working with professionals and entrepreneurs nationwide, helping them build their dreams, accelerate their results and create richer, more fulfilling lives.

Felicia's workshops and coaching programs help people breakthrough limitations and achieve greater results than they've ever known before.

Felicia also specialises in helping people who feel stuck and dissatisfied with their lives, so they can quicky get unstuck, build their dreams and enjoy a more productive and fulfilling life epxerience.

"*Sometimes, changing one thing, changes everything.*"

- Susan Lord -

HAPPINESSLAND

"You should work in an office. That's your best option." the Career Advisor said to me. I didn't disagree with her. I'd had so many different ideas for jobs that I thought I wanted to do, like being a nurse, an air hostess or a fashion designer but I always changed my mind and here I was, a 16-year-old about to break out into the world. The bottom line was I needed to earn money so I decided, that to work in an office, might not have been a bad idea at all.

I reminisce now at how I always told myself to put on my happy face before I left Monae at nursery every day or dropped Nathan off at school club every morning, kissing them both goodbye and greeted other parents, again with my happy face. Then, as soon as I'd drive away to go home and get ready for work, I'd cry uncontrollably for a good few minutes, before realising I needed to catch a bus to work.

Once I'd approach the Children's Hospital, just over an hour later, my chest would tighten and my hands would start to tremble. Although I never wanted to enter, I knew that I had to, so I would swallow hard on the lump in my throat, swipe my access card and my trembling hands would push open the doors. Again, I'd try to put on my happy face but it would leave my face just as soon as it got there. Darkness would suddenly descend and my head would go fuzzy from not being able to think straight. Feelings of dread would shroud me and my body would slump as I grudgingly realised every day that I was going through the motions because I had to and not because I wanted to.

Angela, my colleague and I would talk about what had gone wrong from the previous day and what was likely to go wrong that day. I'd check my emails whilst we did this and never failed to panic every time I realised I had up to sixty emails to deal with. I'd sit there dumbfounded, hit again by the feeling that I was exactly where I was not supposed to be, doing what I was not meant to be doing. There had to be something better for me to do than this. My stern boss, barking dozens of orders, harassing me over what might not have been accomplished didn't make things any better. We spent our days moaning about how unreasonable and unfair she really was.

To make matters worse, I'd be alone once I'd tucked the children into bed because my husband Paul was usually away on business in the Czech Republic. I'd cry again for another thirty odd minutes rocking myself for comfort, tears streaming down my face and then eventually, the tears would abate. This went on for five years.

I'd often ask myself what I wanted and every time I'd reply to myself that what I wanted was to live in Happinessland. I'd ask myself where Happinessland was, what it would be like and the reply always came that it would be the place where I would feel completely fulfilled and live life on my own terms. I'd be in the best of health there, doing a job I absolutely loved and I'd have purpose. I'd be surrounded by people who love and support me and I'd feel pure joy. Every time I thought about Happinessland, a sense of calm would descend and I would feel completely content. The question remained, "How do I get to Happinessland?"

I realised that if I was to get to Happinessland, I had to be brutally honest with myself. I had to identify my passion and what I was good at, which was self-development, inspiring and motivating people to change. This was the area I researched to see what opportunities there were.

Then the universe conspired to put things together for me. I kept seeing adverts to train as a Health and Life Coach, over and over again. Having dealt with a number of health issues myself, I decided to take a look, and I knew instantly that this was my path. My soul felt at peace, like nothing I had felt before. As a Health and Life Coach, I had purpose.

I did the course, worked on my mindset and developing myself, read a ton of books and listened to self-help mentors like Oprah and Brendon Burchard.

And then I made a massive decision and left my job.

Fast forward to today, I can't help but giggle when I'm asked what it is that I do? I proudly say that I'm a Health and Life Coach, helping people who are going through depression, stress, anxiety, emotional eating disorders, sugar and food addiction or want to redesign their lives so it's aligned to their purpose. I specialise in these subjects, as they are issues that I have personally been through myself.

People often want to know more about me, how I reached my goal through self-development, how I got myself out into the world to discover it, how I overcame my fears and how I stepped out of my comfort zone. They realise that I learned lessons from every challenging experience, made difficult decisions and faced my fears head on.

What I want to tell all children is to follow their dreams above anything else. This is a message I consistently give to my own children as well. And if they don't have a dream, I want to tell them to go out and experience the world and when their dream appears, follow that path and not let anyone sway them from it.

SUSAN LORD

TRANSFORMATIONAL HEALTH AND LIFE COACH

facebook.com/Happinessland1

Susan Lord is a Transformational Health and Life Coach. She is on a mission to empower 10 million people around the world to transform their lives and their health.

She does this by creating new habits and a strong mindset with her clients that will enable them to manage chronic health conditions and live a life free of pain, increase energy, reduce stress and anxiety, feel vibrant and find balance and authenticity in their lives.

Susan is also a regular contributor to Childcare Biz Chat Magazine. Susan Lord is passionate about her mission after having overcome chronic health issues herself.

"Yes, you still have your wobbles, your moments or doubt. I still stamp my feet and have times when I question if it is all worth it. But my darling I promise it is! Nothing is more powerful than living in your truth."

- Claire MacPherson -

LIVING IN YOUR TRUTH

I used to worry that I didn't have that 'powerful' story you see entrepreneurs share on stages. You know the ones that shock you or rock you to the core?

Now that isn't to say that I don't have stories, and it certainly isn't to say this has been an easy journey. I think as change makers, as people who want to go out into the world and shine our light brightly, we can fall into the trap of thinking we need the rags to riches story or the heartbreak to happiness, or something else that we feel we just don't have.

It's that little voice of judgment that can creep into our heads and hold us back in any way that it can.

Mine is the story of the girl who probably created most of her problems herself, the story of a girl who grew up with so much love and support from amazing parents and grandparents, also the story of a girl who always felt inside that she wasn't doing a good enough job. The story of a girl who for so long, put pleasing others before pleasing herself.

Sounds like a familiar story? Well of course, and here's the magic about sharing something we all experience at times.

You start to realise that actually, you can still achieve greatness yourself. You see that you are not alone with that voice in your head that might be filled with self doubt, that you're not the only one trying to glide gracefully over the troubled waters like a swan, when beneath you are kicking madly to stay afloat.

So yes, I had a fabulous family and had a good childhood. I had a massive imagination and spent lots of time daydreaming. Every chance I got unwatched, I would jump off things, like the back of a sofa or the stairs because I was convinced that I could fly. In my dreams I could always fly.

In all my school years, all my energy went into trying to fit in, trying to be a part of the crowd, and even more so, trying to be the cool girl who had her own cool little gang. I did pretty well at school, but I could have done so much better. This 'trying to fit in' behaviour continued into university and then to my first teaching job.

The designer clothes, bags, shoes and sports car, all evidence of me desperately trying to find my place in the world and be liked, thinking this would make me happy. However, inside there was always a space. On nights out I would escape to the bathroom just to get away from it all, I would be the fun girl at parties but had no one I felt I could truly share how I was feeling with.

I did find my happiness, with my husband and two boys born just 13 months apart, it was all a huge change, one that rocked my world and one that began the process of me actually starting to discover who I really was. This led to 10 years of total craziness, I left teaching and set up a children's play centre and soon moved to New Zealand because of my husband's job. That was an amazing adventure and my soul did need more. I looked to my purpose and that led me to coaching which was a big step forward into discovering myself.

Five years later the universe decided it was time to kick my ass! We moved back to the UK for a job that soon disappeared and this left us at odds with what to do for a living. At this point we'd had another child, my daughter just being a few months old and things naturally got difficult financially. My eldest son was diagnosed with Aspergers ASD and that presented an even bigger challenge.

I did start up a coaching practice but things were so different in the UK. It seemed like the market was saturated and competition was stiff. I decided to take my business online and had no idea where to start. I would sit and watch free webinars, each promising me that this was the secret I was looking for. I would do it all, invest in more courses, but I still had just a handful of low paying clients.

My husband decided to fulfill his dream of opening up a fish and chips shop. We borrowed money to start it up and another nightmare came to our doorstep. Instead of it being the income we needed, it drained us even more. Quality family time suffered due to long working hours. Paying the mortgage presented bigger challenges also. I was trying to juggle everything but it felt like nothing was working.

At odds, anger and resentment building up, I snapped to attention one day and resolved to change things. I realised that deep down I was in a total place of scarcity. I was trying to do everything 'right', copying all the experts, rather than showing the world who I really was. I was waiting to be magically rescued and that was just not happening.

I made the decision that I needed to "be" the change and "make" the difference, that I needed to play a bigger game and start really showing up in my business.

And guess what, things started to change!

I put up my prices, got more visible, started thinking, feeling and behaving as the fully booked coach that I wanted to be - and from this place, clients started to say YES! I soon saw my first 5k month and massive change happened over the next few years. Hitting my first 20k month was magical, something I never dreamed possible for me.

The most powerful part of this journey was discovering who I really am, taking off the mask, leaving behind the need to please those around me, and the permission I gave myself simply to show up and be ME!

CLAIRE MACPHERSON

MINDSET AND BUSINESS GROWTH COACH

clairemacpherson.com

Claire Macpherson is a mindset and business growth coach for purpose driven women wanting to grow a business they feel passionate about. Over the past ten years, as a coach, speaker and trainer, Claire has helped thousands of women take the first steps in making their businesses a successful reality supporting them both with the mindset and strategy to hit their first five figure months and beyond. Claire's philosophy is "soul before strategy", meaning that when we show up authentically, share from our soul, and really embrace our gifts, talents and journey in our business, we magnetically attract ideal clients to us.

For Claire, having a business that feels fun, fabulous and freeing is key and in this energy, she helps women unleash their uniqueness, create a powerful message and get visible for those soul clients who need them.

"Whatever you do, do it with love,
from a place of love.
Success is guaranteed."

- Kalyani Pardeshi -

HOW RECURRING FAILURES HELPED ME LEARN THE GREATEST LESSON IN LIFE

Around eight years ago, I made a crucial decision that turned my life around one hundred and eighty degrees. I really had no idea what was in store for me when I took the decision as it seemed to be one of the most common decisions women make. Why would it be any different for me? I quit my career in finance to raise my two young children. I resigned from my job as a financial analyst just six weeks shy of the birth of my son, my second child.

The first few months were difficult as it is for any mother trying to master a balancing act between two very young children. What added to my difficulties were the health problems my son faced - breast milk jaundice, suspected asthma, weight gaining issues, roseola, incessant ear infections and gag reflex to name just a few. I was drained and didn't admit to anyone that I was silently battling postpartum depression.

I finally found the courage to open up to a doctor about my depression. What he said shook me to the core. "It isn't about you anymore," his words thundered in my ears. I felt alone and terrified, totally unsure of where to pick up the pieces and attempt to move forward. I had been going to the gym, more for social interaction than to burn calories. A friend I had made there, recommended I read The Secret by Rhonda Byrne. I finally took her advice.

Slowly things started turning around for me but there was still an emptiness I felt within myself. This emptiness was aggravated by criticism directed at me from those, whom I thought I could depend on unconditionally. Apparently not. According to them, nothing I did was right - not the way I raised my children, not the way I took care of my home. The list was endless and the implication was that I was not good enough.

Anger and frustration drove me in futile attempts to prove them wrong. I decided to join an MLM (Multilevel Marketing Company) to become an entrepreneur. My intention was to become so successful that my critics would eat their words. I worked hard, night and day, slaved away, did everything imaginable to see the kind of success I had dreamt of, to see the look of shame and embarrassment on the faces of my critics once I succeeded. However, that was a dream out of my reach. A year after joining the MLM, I had to quit as I wasn't breaking even.

I convinced myself this was because the programs sold by the MLM weren't available in the countries where women contacted me from, so I figured I could create my own programs to cater to their needs. I could already taste immense success. And again, I dove in, head first, worked weekends this time as well, worked my skin to the bone, did everything in my power to see the kind of success I pictured - all with intention to make my critics eat their words. My family life suffered, I wasn't able to give my children and my husband the kind of time I used to before. I kept telling myself how worth the success would be, I imagined rubbing my success in the faces of my critics.

Unfortunately, after two years of labouring away, I couldn't birth the kind of success I dreamt of. Though I was making some money, it wasn't nearly enough to break even. I was drained, exhausted and defeated. My critics had won, maybe I wasn't "good enough" after all. I closed my second business down in April 2017 and I took some time off.

I figured that if not a business, I can find work from home job opportunities and make a roaring success out of it. Armed with a new plan of action, I dedicated myself over the next few months, applying for every work from home job that promised a fixed income. At this point, I would like to mention that I come from a culture which recognises you for your achievements and not for who you are, the basis of which I was criticised - I wasn't doing anything except raising my children and wasn't achieving anything, hence I was a "nobody". The fact that I helped my son in overcoming every struggle of his including teaching him how to talk and read by the time he was four, was written off by my critics as a mother's responsibility and nothing special worth commending. Why was this a huge achievement for me? My son didn't utter a single coherent word at two and half years of age, not even "mama".

I was rejected for every single job I applied for. I felt defeated and started sliding into depression again. I felt worthless, questioning everything I believed in. Up until now, I had always used negative criticism as a source of motivation to drive me to succeed and until now, I had always succeeded using this technique. After all, this is exactly how I lost 60lbs after my second pregnancy.

Seven months into this downward spiral, I received Katrina Ruth's course, "High Level Manifestation," as a gift. As with anything else, I was skeptical at first but just one lesson in that course cleared the fog of self-doubt in an instant. The lesson was about alignment of goals with core values. Basically, if your goals are not aligned with your core values, you will not succeed in those goals. This made so much sense!

My ultimate core value is self-respect. And no self-respecting individual needs to prove their worth or value to anyone. The reason I succeeded in losing weight was because my goal of losing weight wasn't clashing with my core value of self-respect. This explained why I had succeeded at every venture in the past when I was driven by negative criticism. My goals were never in conflict with my self-respect. But ultimately, trying to prove my worth and value went against everything I hold dear to me because of my core value of self-respect. Hence my lack of success.

This lesson has enabled me to do a "gut check" every time I choose to do something - is it coming from a place of love or is it coming from a place to prove someone wrong? If it is the latter, I drop the idea altogether, no matter how enticing it may be.

KALYANI PARDESHI

AUTHOR, ANTI-BULLYING ADVOCATE

facebook.com/kalyanispeaks

Kalyani Pardeshi is a CPA based in Canada who is an avid anti-bullying advocate. In 2010, she quit her career to raise her kids. One consistent theme in her life was that wherever, she went, bullying followed her and she refused to be broken down by her tormentors.

She self-developed tools to help her not only cope instead thrive despite the bullying, while also using it as fuel to motivate her to greater success. She uses her experiences and what she has learnt from them to equip teenagers with tools of their own to overcome the scars of bullying because she firmly believes that it is easier to mold a child than it is to mend an adult.

"We can change our pain to passion and purpose by transforming challenges into lessons and propelling ourselves into lives we will be proud to live and share. It's never a breakdown it's a metamorphosis."

- Victoria Powell -

FROM THE ABYSS
TO THE ART OF
SOUL LIBERATION

Born and raised in Bristol, an A grade student, popular with amazing friends, and dreams to pursue a career in the arts, there was no telling that in my teens I would suddenly suffer the aftermath of the divorce of my parents from way back when I was just six years old. I suffered chronic fatigue, depression and anxiety and within a few years became a shadow of my original self. I can't quite articulate what those years of my life were like except to say that they were crippling and began to define who I was. A dark shadow thwarted my ambitions and cast a damp spirit on my soul. Friendships lost, I became a recluse with erratic behaviour patterns that seemed to spiral out of control. I couldn't afford all of the treatment that I would need to get well fully and allowed myself to fall into the deep dark abyss that waited for me as I sunk deeper and deeper.

Although I made a slight recovery in my late twenties and went on to flourish in a great corporate career, I still felt unfulfilled. My heart and soul yearned for something more and try as I might, I could not put my finger on it. As I moved on into my thirties, the feeling of being stifled and unfulfilled still lingered. On paper, I was thriving, but my personal life was still suffering. Stuck in a toxic relationship for a long time, I could not accept that the bond between my boyfriend and I had reached its tethers end. As I continued to hang on to what was left of it, I starved myself of any loving relationship I could have been in, had I just realised that I didn't need him to validate that I was a whole, beautiful woman. I lacked so much of self-esteem that I accepted the shreds of love and attention I got, but craved so much more. When all aspects of my life began to suffer as a result of the fledgling relationship, I finally let go.

You would think that I would have started to feel better when I did this. Instead, I started to suffer extreme social anxiety. I turned to various unhealthy mechanisms to cope and took it a step further by mixing medication with alcohol. Although it masked the anxiety and depression for a little while, I began to hate who I was becoming and began to behave irrationally on many levels. The realisation that my boyfriend of 12 years was not coming back dawned on me and I finally had my first breakdown. Suicidal, numb and empty, I took a huge dose of tablets with alcohol as a 'cry for help' and as a way to escape and numb my pain. I believed that I didn't deserve to live.

The awakening on the other side of my accidental overdose suddenly had me feeling lucky and blessed to be alive. Something within me felt light and I felt like I was ready to give myself another shot at living. Feelings of deserving better, self respect and yearning to grow into the best version of myself overtook my senses and I suddenly felt a kind of self-love that is hard to convey and articulate.

I took control of my mental health and post traumatic stress disorder and started a difficult but empowering journey back to myself and wellness. I became my own best friend. I learned to feel my feelings however painful they were and dealt with the decades of pain that had been entrenched within my body mind and soul. Before I took my steps to recovery and self-enlightenment, I had to do one major thing: to forgive myself, release all the shame, guilt and regret - instead live in gratitude and growth.

I got out of my comfort zone and joined some online self help groups where I could engage and talk to others who really empathised with me and didn't judge me. I also started writing, journaling and singing again. I felt relieved and the burden started to lift. I continued to keep making steps towards my recovery and slowly learned to love myself again.

Doing better, by 2016 I had landed an amazing corporate job with a fantastic salary, however there was still the inner feeling that I was destined for a different path. No amount of effort could help me determine what it was I sought, until I immersed myself in self development programmes that saw me letting go of what was and focus on what is. I have an incredible spirit and hunger for helping people and when I finally discovered that this was my calling, I stopped feeling like I was living an empty life. I finally felt the joy and purpose I had always craved. As I learned and made new likeminded friends, the more the opportunities to help others through self development arose, and I began to enjoy living again. I still have moments in which I am vulnerable and am afraid to share too much about myself with others and I am still grateful for the journey, it's lesson and the chance to live my life fully all over again.

Fate will deal you many heavy hands but each one has a reason and a lesson. It is my absolute pleasure to teach women how to connect with their authentic selves and how to cope when things become too overwhelming. By doing this, I help ladies avoid the pitfalls I fell into during my own journey and I am so happy when they too learn the art of converting traumatic events into transformational and empowering learning experiences.

VICTORIA POWELL

THE MIND METAMORPHOSIS COACH

facebook.com/MindMetamorphosis

Victoria appeared to have the dream life with a high-flying corporate position in Dublin's fair city for many years, but she was masking her deep ridden anxiety issues. Through self-development she experienced a metamorphosis in mindset.

She now coaches women to catalyse their own transformation from social anxiety to a true sense of self. As a qualified Reiki Practitioner and through her own mind metamorphosis techniques and strategies, which she developed over the years, she is now able to touch lives in effective and innovative ways.

"Although your journey may be long, never forget your destination and you will find your way. The twists and turns will enrich your path and add to your wisdom. Never give up and don't let the limitations define you."

- Gloria Prest -

FINDING MY WAY

I cannot start my story with a litany of woes because I was born into a loving family. I never experienced scarcity, abuse or neglect. Nonetheless, I did suffer from the misogynistic treatment inflicted on most girls of my age and social circumstances. During the last years of the Spanish dictatorship under General Franco, being female was a severe disadvantage. Most women, like my mother, worked more than men but had less freedom and less power. Women worked alongside the men in the factories or on the land, and then, did all of the domestic chores and childcare as well. Yet, it was the men who were the "heads of the household" and who made the decisions. Even as a young child this disparity burned deeply within my soul and never more than when I was denied the opportunity to continue pursuing a higher education because I was a girl. When I finished my national school education, age 14, I went straight to work. My father said that if I wanted to continue studying, it would have to be on my own time. He was not willing to support me while I studied. He was going to pay for my brother's studies, but not mine, because I was a girl.

I was very disappointed because I was a very good student. I had a zest for learning, however my parents, who were semiliterate, did not value education. I did! I knew that education would be my way to a life different from theirs. They had a neighbourhood shop, that was open 7 days a week, 15 hours a day. We lived at the back of the shop and work took priority over family life. I worked in that shop after school and at weekends from the day that I was tall enough to be seen behind the counter. Then, full time 7 days a week from when I left school. What I wanted was a well-paid 9-5 job. Yes, that is right! I wanted the kind of job that people nowadays complain about and dream of leaving behind. You see, working only 8 hours a day and having free weekends was a dream of mine. I knew that without any further qualifications I would not be able to get such a job. Therefore, I decided that I would go to night school. I was determined.

Unfortunately, I was unaware that schools like mine, did not give you access to apply for higher education. I was bitterly disappointed that my schooling had come to an educational dead end. I was angry but not deterred. I had to resign myself to do two years of evening study just to be able to get entry to the next level, which I did. By then, however, I was working in a factory, and I found the ten-hour shifts of physical labour were not conducive to following academic pursuits. My education was on hold again. Still, Lady Luck seemed to smile on me when I unexpectedly got the opportunity to study after being made redundant. I was gutted to lose my job, but the generous redundancy package allowed me to pay for a full-time one-year course in pre-school education. I successfully completed the course, but my thirst for learning was not satisfied. I was 19 and very impatient to see the world. I decided to go to the UK as an au-pair and learn English. However, the agency painted such a black picture of life in the UK that I decided to go to Italy instead. During my time there I made up my mind that I had to go to University. When I returned, I went back to working in the family business and started the Baccalaureate at night school. After a full day's work, depleted, I travelled to the next town where I attended college. I remember arriving back home around 11 o'clock at night, exhausted, and having to cook my own dinner. While my brother was waited on hand and foot, never having to lift a finger at home, I was fending for myself on all levels.

Through sheer perseverance and hard work, I finished my baccalaureate and went to Granada University. Sadly, after successfully completing the first year, of a three-year degree in Translation, circumstances required me to abandon my studies, and I moved to the UK.

Years later, I was married, and my first child was diagnosed with profound deafness and unspecified developmental difficulties. I again felt the burning need to study more, to learn more, this time out of necessity. No one can imagine the challenges that came with raising a deaf child with additional unspecified needs. We saw many experts, but none were able to give an adequate diagnosis and often gave us completely contradicting advice. Hence, I embarked on my own research to learn about deafness, language acquisition, coordination disorders, dyslexia, sensory processing, developmental issues, etc.

Eventually, I succeeded in having him diagnosed with Dyspraxia and Asperger's Syndrome, and I fought to find the best support for him. My learning curve was huge, and with it came clarity about what I wanted to study. You can say I finally found my "reason" and my "why". I wanted to put all that I had learned independently, into a more formal scientific framework. At age 45, I enrolled for a Psychology degree and enjoyed every minute of every lecture because I had earned the right to be there. I finally studied something for which I was truly passionate. Now, I work as a psychotherapist and hypnotherapist. More importantly, I provide the kind of psychological information for parents that I wished I had at the time I was facing challenges.

GLORIA PREST

COUNSELLOR AND HYPNOTHERAPIST

mindinfocus.co.uk

Gloria Prest is a successful Counsellor and Hypnotherapist. She is fascinated by the science underpinning the brain and mind functionality and has a way of making the information accessible and easy for anyone to understand.

Her success therefore lies in helping people to improve the way they think and feel. Having had personal and professional experience in working with children with developmental and emotional difficulties, Gloria also helps parents to understand their children's minds and supports them with development and learning.

"When we take responsibility for our health and wellbeing, we show up as the best version of ourselves and we reap the benefit in all areas of our lives."

- Sue Ritchie -

MY JOURNEY FROM PAIN TO PROSPERITY

A few years ago and for too many years of my life, I was a part of the "Overworked and Frantic People Club." However, I discovered after a huge health wake-up call that the Club doesn't recruit you, you choose to join it of your own volition. It may not be a conscious decision, however it is nonetheless easy to get yourself sucked into over a period of time. The great thing about this, is that you can choose to resign from the 'Club'. You have that power in your hands.

I was brought up to believe, that in order to be successful you had to work hard. And boy did I take that on board big time!

My whole working life up until about 7 years ago, was one where I was constantly on that treadmill, working long hours, looking after everyone else, and not looking after me. Over the years I gradually gave up on all the things that I loved to do, like craft, photography, singing and dancing. There was no time to do them. My social life was limited to weekends. Many times I arranged to meet friends after work and then cancelled at the last minute. There really wasn't any time for fun.

Typically, I'd be working on deadline driven projects that had an almost immediate turnaround time. During the day I'd often be interrupted by others wanting me to help them out on other tasks and because I wasn't assertive enough to say 'no', the work day would soon be over and I'd work overtime on my own tasks in order to meet project deadlines. I was after all an achiever and not a shirker.

I left my successful corporate career to start my own business on the premise that I would have more flexibility and I could spend more time with my two children. That worked for a couple of years and then the old patterns returned. I'd find myself working after the children had gone to bed. Sometimes I'd stay up until 2am to get things finished and then be up again at 7am to get the children ready for school.

Then 7 years ago, I found myself struggling with fatigue, brain fog, difficulty focusing and concentrating, joint pain, difficulty sleeping, anxiety and a weight problem. It didn't matter what I did, the weight just wouldn't reduce. This all had a huge impact on my business as well as my personal life. There were days when I thought that I was literally going mad.

I was diagnosed with Hashimoto's disease (an autoimmune disease that affects the thyroid gland), left the doctors surgery with a prescription in my hand and the determination to do everything possible to get myself totally well again. Why?

When I received the diagnosis, I asked if I could get well again, I was told in no uncertain terms that it was impossible and I would be on the medication for the rest of my life. I was shocked. As I took in what the doctor had said, there were several things that went through my head as I tried to make sense of it all.

Am I really going to have to put up with feeling as bad as I do for the rest of my life? I didn't want to feel the way I was for another 30 or more years and because I had generally lived an active life, I did not want to accept what the doctor was saying. There were lots of things I still wanted to achieve. I loved travelling to different parts of the world, meeting new people, learning about different cultures and I wanted to do so much more of that. I was looking forward to the prospect of running around after my grandchildren and having fun, if I was blessed with any. I love taking walks in nature, swimming and dancing. Was I never going to be able to do any of these things again? The thought of living any less of a life was just unacceptable to me.

I started researching my condition to find out the root causes and I made some big life changing decisions. I stepped off of the treadmill, started to take time out for myself, took care of myself and I created a much better work life balance. Did my business implode? No. In fact I doubled my turnover and almost doubled my profit, because putting solid work time boundaries in place meant I worked smarter not harder.

I discovered that the root cause of my Hashimoto's disease and other autoimmune diseases lay in my gut health. So I went through a process to rebalance my gut microbiome and made changes to my diet. Within weeks I got my energy back and felt so much better. I lost 2.5 stone in 3 months and within 18 months I was off medication and recovered from the Hashimoto's disease.

The gifts and the lessons that came from this situation were that we are all responsible for our own health. We ought to put ourselves first and make big decisions based purely on what we want and not what others want. We should not work hard to be successful but rather work smarter. We must take good care of ourselves and make sure we are satisfied. We ought to do the things we love, which make us feel good without feeling guilty. It's okay to ask for help and if we did, we wouldn't run ourselves into the ground. Self care is about setting our boundaries and keeping them intact.

The real gift that came from my experience and lessons is that I now help others to get off the treadmill and to rebalance, refocus, revitalise and start living their lives to the full.

SUE RITCHIE

COACH, SPEAKER AND AUTHOR

sue-ritchie.com

Sue Ritchie is passionate about helping stressed out female entrepreneurs and professionals that are busting their guts to re-balance revitalise and re-focus their lives whilst boosting their success.

Sue's previous life involved working long hours under high levels of stress. She was constantly pushing herself to the limit, trying to fit everything in. A big health wake-up call resulted in a decision to create a better work life balance, resulting in one of the most successful years in her business, doubling her revenue and profit. Sue is a coach, speaker and author of an award winning book, 'Love your Gut: The Practical Guide to Successful Weight Loss from the Inside Out'.

"Read, breathe and release.
I release all blocks preventing me from
having faith in myself."

- Faith Rodriguez -

HAVING FAITH

When my mum was pregnant with me, she had faith that I was a girl. She already had my two older brothers; hence really wanted a girl. She was told that I was a boy, but she just knew that they were wrong. So, when I was born she named me Faith, for all the faith she had in me being a girl, her girl.

At an early age, I started to notice energy and I could feel when the energy or aura in a room changed. I would go from feeling safe and comfortable to feeling as if I was being watched which made me feel scared. One night I woke up with that feeling, so I turned on my ceiling light, then laid back down and fell asleep. I woke up soon after, my sleep disrupted by a male voice talking to me. When I opened my eyes, there was a man floating in the middle of my room, grey smoke exuding from his waist down.

I froze in disbelief wondering if it was all a dream, however it didn't go away. So I sat up, terrified, seeing him as clear as day. With my eyes glued on the male figure, I got out of bed. With my back against the wall, I slid along to the doorway, then ran down the hall to my parents' room. I woke my mum up and told her what had just happened. She said I must have had a bad dream.

When I was six years old, my dad who was in the army, got orders to be stationed in Germany. Upon arrival, our housing wasn't ready, so we were placed in a beautiful guest house out in the country. Our family became good friends with the owners of the guest house. When we could, my brothers Thomas, Joseph, Oliver and I would explore the woods, especially all the places that were off limits. One afternoon as I was standing on the patio in front of the guest house, I had a vision of my brother Joe. In my vision, he was standing in the garden with a shovel. A snake was in front of him, curled up ready to strike. Tom's hollering voice jolted me out of my vision. We ran to find out what was wrong. What Joe described had me covered in goose bumps. It was exactly what I saw in my vision.

I shared this with my mum, shocking her. Truth be told, I feel she didn't know what to say. This was the early eighties, a time when things like these weren't openly discussed. I later found out that my grandmother was very intuitive while both my parents had seen spirits. I had many similar experiences throughout my life, irrespective of where I lived. At the time, I tried to block out sensing the energy of emotions of other people around me. I didn't want to be different. Like anyone else, I wanted to be accepted, I wanted to fit in.

As time went on, I kept denying my gifts as profusely as I possibly could. I was now happily married with two daughters and a son, all of whom are intuitive. After having my son, I started experiencing more spiritual encounters. By then, I was good at reading energy and recognizing it either as safe and loving, or not. If the energy was negative I would pray for the energy to be removed. I had faith that if I did this, then I would be safe and I always was. I used to be an introvert and often held onto my emotions. I shared my experiences with my husband and immediate family only. Holding onto my emotions led to health issues. When I was in my early twenties I was diagnosed with rheumatoid arthritis and in my early thirties, endometriosis, resulting in requiring a hysterectomy.

When I was thirty-five my kids were in the third, seventh, and ninth grades respectively. I was a 'stay at home mum' and at the time, it was my first year of homeschooling my kids. I kept feeling that I was supposed to be a part of something bigger. That feeling didn't go away. It kept getting stronger and stronger. So strong, that one day while vacuuming my living room floor, I dropped the vacuum hose while the vacuum was still running, I looked up, spread my arms in sheer exasperation, hollering to no one in particular, "Then what am I to do? If I'm supposed to do something bigger, what is it?"

Two days later my kids were scheduled to undergo state testing. I chose to volunteer at the testing site. There I met a wonderful woman by the name of Monica. I had never met a medium before. She had answers to so many questions, answers which changed my life forever. Monica went on to become my first spiritual teacher, quickly changing my life in magical ways. I read books, took spiritual development classes, I learned about angels, energy healing and meditation. Within a month of exercising healing on myself and releasing the energy around the emotions I was holding onto, I no longer needed medication for the rheumatoid arthritis or for any other pain.

By word of mouth, my work spread. I started offering different types of sessions and teaching spiritual development classes. I volunteered intuitive information on missing person cases. Today, I am known as a professional international Psychic Medium, Energy Healer and Intuitive mentor who works with people from all over the world. I love using my intuition to help others as it fills my heart with love while truly bringing me healing. My favourite student is my granddaughter Aurora Faith who brings love, joy and inspiration into my life. Her intuitive skills never cease to amaze me and the clarity she has is truly magical. Many people have faith in me, thus making my journey magical. I bring this love into my sessions helping others to have faith in themselves. May your journey be filled with faith, love and blessings.

FAITH RODRIGUEZ

PSYCHIC MEDIUM, ENERGY HEALER
AND INTUITIVE MENTOR

faithrodriguez.net

Faith Rodriguez is an international Psychic Medium, Energy Healer and Intuitive Mentor. She offers different types of sessions promoting healing. Through her private sessions, in-person or online sessions, Faith has worked with intuitive children and adults, helping them understand and fine tune their intuition. She shares spirit messages, bringing peace and closure after a loss including connecting with pets that are living and that have passed, sharing their messages with their loved ones.

Faith offers different energy healing sessions and teaches her clients how to channel divine light energy to heal themselves and others. She uses her intuition to mentor others in their businesses, life, relationships and healing. She also teaches different energy clearings to shift energies, promoting healing within the physical, mental, spiritual, emotional and energy bodies.

"Miracles and success come not from overcoming adversity, but from discovering, in adversity, who you really are. You are surely going to discover that you are a piece of Divine awareness."

- Susan Suehr -

THE UNKNOWN ONLY CONTAINS MORE OF THE REAL YOU

We have all heard about people experiencing miracles. However, do you think that they are meant for you or that you need to be in a desperate situation before you are graced with one? For me, having what I wanted, let alone a miracle, always involved struggle. I had fun creating things for sure, and there was always that struggle aspect that pervaded all my success. Hearing stories of how others had so much success following their passions, had me questioning what was wrong with me. I was definitely following my passion but was successively experiencing challenge after challenge.

To me it just seemed as if I had faced challenges all my life. The middle one of 10 other children, I had 2 eye surgeries and narrowly escaped rape at the age of 9. I faced near death at gunpoint too. Normal, right? I didn't think so and I can't help but be cynical about it.

But I was gifted, too. Math, science, and good grades came easily for me. My burning desire to do something special saw me graduate as a Chemical Engineer when discrimination and sexual harassment of female engineers was rampant. My petit body and youthful looks made being taken seriously for management roles practically impossible. I spent 40 years introducing more than

26 medical devices and pharmaceutical products and processes into the marketplace with multiple patents to support them. For everyone else this was a challenge. For me this was something that I was passionate about and it was easy to do, yet I always felt that something was missing. I know most of my products helped people have a better life, yet there wasn't a sense of fulfilment. There was always a niggling feeling that I was missing out on doing something more important with my life and it became frustrating trying to figure out what it was. How do I explain, that although I was grateful for the position that I was in, I was still seeking something more fulfilling.

Little did I know that these years were only preparing me for fulfilling my real purpose. I had many setbacks and had to fight for funding of my projects as well as my patents. You would think, that although my projects had value, they would not face any challenges to implement or get funding for. On the contrary, I faced challenge after challenge, verifying, justifying my work and objectives which was rather daunting. I was involved in 5 downsizings as well. I questioned why making millions of dollars for my company didn't protect me from this? I am convinced that my sheer will, determination, and work integrity is what carried me through successful projects and finding new jobs. Even though I was successful, I had been practicing how to struggle as a way to succeed. I never believed that I could ever be blessed with a miracle. I was just too ordinary and God must have not considered me special enough to have it all.

My last downsizing during a sluggish economy at age 63, made finding another job dismal. So I started my own business doing my second passion which is meditation, spirituality and blogging. I was not prepared for how much hard work it was to get noticed in a high traffic internet market. Here again, I was dealing with struggle. I heal clients who are dealing with trauma and am thriving by word of mouth marketing. Most of all, I believe that I am successful today because I am having the most amount of fun I have ever had in my life.

I have realised what has really helped me through life.

First, I followed my intuition closely and I believe that because I have listened and acted on it, I have been able to make a success of my second innings at a wonderful career. Second, I had let go completely of needing any specific outcome and because I was no longer anxious about succeeding, I exceeded my own expectations in an unforeseen arena at an unexpected age. Thirdly, I accepted who I am completely and stopped being scared to enjoy myself and what I am doing. I have learned to let go of the past and the challenges I faced back then. I have accepted that they are a part of the tests I had to have in order to get to where I am now. I am convinced that a large part of my greatness is as a direct result of the lessons I learned. I no longer question or try to analyse the course of my life and its preceding challenges so closely anymore. They don't keep me awake at night nor are they a preoccupation. I have found my peace in living this way.

At this point in my life, I am acutely aware that I am not the only one who experienced tests or challenges. In fact, there are many people who experience worse than me, so I am blessed for learning from my life events.

SUSAN SUEHR

MEDITATION MASTER AND ENERGY HEALER

ChangeYourBeliefsNow.com

Susan Suehr is a meditation master, also known as an energy healer. She is formally a Chemical Engineer and spiritual healer. She helps other spiritual seekers discover their true selves and make positive changes to themselves in a few weeks.

She has developed an array of products which include meditation that helps people reach that inner peaceful place to receive nudges, to let go of negative beliefs that hold them back, and to completely accept the truth about who they are.

"Follow the joy,
and the rest will follow."

- Sharon Svenson -

MY DEPRESSION LED ME TO JOY

The depression came on suddenly and stayed like an impenetrable fog that wouldn't lift. At the time I was a mother of two toddlers. My husband worked long days or was gone months at a time for jobs, trying to pay our bills. I felt alone with the care and responsibility of my daughters. My eldest had health issues. I dragged her to multiple experts, with no answers. I felt helpless watching her suffer. With no medical insurance, our debt ballooned. I had my own health struggles and was running on fumes, sleep interrupted by a sick child or a daughter's nightmares. On top of that, there was a serial rapist and killer terrorizing our rural area targeting women fitting my profile. I felt vulnerable and afraid.

One morning I woke feeling submerged underwater; movements slow and heavy, senses muted, cut off from the outside world. As I forced myself to move through the day and care for my daughters, things improved. But little events could trigger anxiety; what to cook, a daughter's tantrum or a bill we couldn't pay. The depression felt like it had settled into my bones. My anxieties turned into recurring panic attacks. Sometimes when driving alone, I'd have fleeting impulses to drive off the road. This scared me. I wanted to live because I loved my daughters deeply.

The passing urge was a desire to end the suffering.

Searching for relief, I turned to the spiritual. I began listening to recordings of sermons from Minister Jack Boland, "The greatest gift you can give yourself is joy, not only because of the feeling that goes with it at the moment, but because of the magnificent experience it will draw to you. It will produce wonders in your life." This message spoke to me deeply. However, my fears ran fast and furious, a spigot turned on which I couldn't shut off. How did I get to that joy? I had real problems. With time, Jack's sermons helped me believe I could turn my anxieties to lighter thoughts. He convinced me, fear was really the cause of my misery. He awakened my faith in God, a God there to help, give guidance and answers.

I started by noticing my thoughts. I was surprised at how negative I was, how easily I fell into complaining and victimhood. Over several months, I wrote reams of paper giving voice to my fears, frustrations and anger. It was cathartic. Acknowledging them made me feel lighter and freer. I burned these papers in our wood stove, a declaration I was willing to move past them and make space for the joy.

When I felt fears coming on, I'd chant the Unity prayer of protection "The light of God surrounds us; The love of God enfolds us; The power of God protects us; The presence of God watches over us; Wherever we are, God is!" It helped me feel protected against serial killers, believe there were answers for my daughter's health challenges and trust that somehow our bills would get paid.

I started to understand I could change my thinking. If I stopped to soothe my fears I could stop them from escalating out of control. I learned I could choose my thoughts independently of outside conditions.

I began to ride my stationary bike daily as I listened to his sermons. Exercise helped stop my negative narratives and open me up to the positive. Long ago episodes, that had been buried under my pain, started to surface. Memories came of angelic voices and support I knew as a child.

At age seven, I wandered to the bottom of our five acres, and followed the banks of a surging creek. The fast-moving water enticed me to dip in my rubber booted foot. As I eased one foot into the stream, my boot sank into the mud beneath the water. Within seconds the mud encased it like cement. I grabbed an exposed root, and wondered, "What now?" I wasn't afraid and knew I was no match for the strength of the creek. A sudden beautiful feeling flooded me with a reassuring presence, a powerful feeling of love. I felt my foot gently release like I was being helped out of a slip-on-shoe. It was my angel, a familiar companion since I was age three. This memory deepened my faith and opened me up to new possibilities.

Within a year, the grip of depression loosened and the disconnected feelings faded. Impulses to drive off the road and panic attacks ceased. As a surprising bonus, my health improved. I would later discover Louise Hay and the important role positive thoughts play in our physical health.

My new thoughts generated energy and ideas, which led me to take inspired actions. I started writing children's stories and plucked up the courage to tell them at our local library. I organized a mastermind group. Answers about my daughter's health came as well. Finances improved.

Years later I discovered hypnosis. Hypnotic states accelerated the release of my negative beliefs and thoughts. This altered state allowed me to absorb positive suggestions, and access my inner-wisdom. As a result, I released my allergies and asthma, became free of medications and lost weight. It led me to things I never could have imagined possible. I took up yoga, became a fire dancer, created a successful business I love, Svenson Hypnosis. Now I support others claim healthier, more joyful, and prosperous lives.

I still have negative thoughts and limiting beliefs, but now I use fears and anxieties as guidance, like the discomfort I get when I am too near a hot stove. I back away. I move toward lighter perspectives. I continue to let go of my made-up limitations using hypnosis, and other tools I've learned along the way. As a result I have had more dreams come true, and life keeps getting better.

SHARON SVENSON

HYPNOTHERAPIST

svensonhypnosis.coachesconsole.com

By releasing negative thought patterns, Sharon has let go of social anxiety, depression, binge eating, extra weight, allergies, asthma, migraine headaches and back problems. With the release came fun, energy, creativity and the inspiration to follow her dreams. It led Sharon to learn to play the guitar, write and perform her children's stories, take up yoga, fire dance and create Svenson Hypnosis.

She has worked with over a 1000 clients who have claimed better health, freedom from depression, anxiety, eating issues and addictions. Instead they now make dreams come true. Success stories include and are not limited to writing books, creating successful business, travelling, enjoying life and learning new things.

The possibilities are infinite.

"It is in the thoughts we have absorbed, and the depths of our subconscious mind where our soul connects and governs the vibrations and energy of our being that manifests our experiences. Let go of that which doesn't serve you and allow your creative imagination to bring joy and gratitude into your heart and magic into your life."

- Susanne Wiechert -

OUT OF ADVERSITY COMES CREATIVITY AND BEAUTY

How could I know that the effects of fleeing a war, being torn away from family and being relocated over and over again would have negative ramifications much later on in my life? How could I understand that such effects would bury themselves deeply in my subconscious mind and manifest into behavioural patterns that would hinder me later on in life?

My childhood memories are actually pleasant. I felt very loved and secure and everything in life seemed abundant. I was aware to some degree of what was going on but I don't recall adversity. Whatever the effects were, they didn't take shape or form immediately.

It was as a young travelling adult, that I discovered a world outside the 'protective zone', which I lived in with my parents. New encounters whilst travelling, had me facing different and sometimes dangerous choices. Meeting people who took drugs as if it was just the norm was something I couldn't relate to but accepted as what 'they' did. Somehow my intuition always kept me safe but one of those people was a tall, handsome man, with whom I fell in love. I was naïve enough to think that in time, his behaviour and habits would change. Being understanding and compassionate by nature, I have always looked for the best in people.

Once married and settled back in the UK, I was in happy oblivion until the vicious cycle that comes with having an addicted partner returns and takes its toll. No longer in control of my emotions, I would sometimes walk the streets with tears streaming down my face, not seeing who or what was around me, my throat closing up, my stomach in knots.

My son's health also deteriorated. At just 14 months he'd had his first asthma attack and by age 4, he was suffering with allergies too. Conventional medicine was only fire-fighting his symptoms and then he'd be back in hospital. I often wondered if our child was ill because he had subconsciously absorbed the effects of the rollercoaster lifestyle we were experiencing.

We had a little reprieve when I started using a liquid nutritional product, recommended by a friend. I was curious and put it to the test for the whole family. With further advice from a nutritionist, I could hardly believe the difference it had made in just six months.

From that point on, I studied Nutrition, Reiki and Bio-Energetics. I was so happy to have 'fixed' things, or so I thought. My son was better, however within a few years, my daughter became ill with severe Fibromyalgia. What was I missing from the equation?

By this time, I had begun to treat others with alternative healing. It was time to make it 'official' and in January 2005, I launched EnergiZeMe, a holistic health practice.

In May of 2008, I decided to complete my 'circle' of health practices with a Master Practitioner course in NLP, neurological re-patterning and results coaching. I wanted to help my family more and also had the idea to approach the corporate world with health and wellness workshops in the workplace. By this time, I had also accepted that no matter how much I wanted to 'fix' things for my partner, how much I believed in him, his addictive patterns would return again and again until he believed enough in himself to do what needed to be done.

Our separation and eventual divorce brought new turmoil, heartache and challenges. It also brought new lessons. Fending for my family was challenging and with the financial crash on the doorstep, I went back into employment in 2010 and worked at my business part-time.

Despite learning new, relevant skills, I found myself being bullied in the workplace. Typical of modern-day working environments, I felt undervalued; my self-worth at an all-time low. I was burning out and experiencing anxiety and depression, allowing myself to be treated badly. This had a certain 'ring' to it. Had I not just come out of a marriage that made me feel like that? Was there something deep in my subconscious I had not resolved?

My intuition kicked in and I knew it was time to leave my job. Energy healing, coaching and meditation to help me 'release', was what I needed. All this led me to a spiritual experience with a pressing desire to express myself creatively. Intuitively and in a meditative state, I began painting out my emotions, my visions and I infused them with healing energy.

I went back to building my business and what makes my heart sing. I was so happy to again be helping others create healthy and empowering change in their lives. This was my purpose and SuzanA was born of my art, paving the way to provide a new source of healing, energy and inspiration for others too.

Enriching the lives of those suffering from stress and stagnation, guiding them to find a way out of their darkness to step into their glorious light, brings such great rewards to all. Whether working one-to-one or with a group or organisation, it has been and continues to be wonderful. Especially to witness the smiles and the revelations that my clients express through the unique combination and flow of my work, as well as to see the power and pleasure that creative expression gives them.

Out of adversity, we can learn and evolve so much. We are creative, spiritual beings in human form with powerful intuition and mind. I urge you to listen carefully to both your inner and outer voice, remain true to your heart, ask for help when you need it and keep faith in yourself.

SUSANNE WIECHERT

EMPOWERMENT AND RESILIENCE COACH

energizeme.co.uk

Susanne Wiechert is a creative and inspiring change-maker, that will ignite your inner health champion and inspire you in unconventional ways.

With a love for variety in life, Susanne offers a unique combination of services that integrate creative flair with professional magnanimity. With a practice in Nutrition, Energy Medicine, NLP and Behaviour Re-patterning, she recently branched out embracing intuitive art, which has greatly influenced her therapy, training and coaching.

Susanne is working on various projects, including developing her art further. She has been a big 'hit' with her Mindfulness, Resilience & Empowerment programmes for employees of her local Council.

"As women, we often feel guilty and selfish for wanting to have it all and put ourselves first. It is vital that we shift our mind-space and start giving importance to ourselves. When we achieve a balance, everything else is possible."

- Sister Zeph -

HOW MY DETERMINATION CHANGED MY DESTINY

Just like any other child, I was a naughty girl. I loved being a leader in my school and dreamt of becoming a lawyer. I was barely thirteen years old when I wrote my first article on women's rights which was published in the Daily Jung in Pakistan, a very well-read newspaper. Like every mother in my country, mine told me what others told their daughters - one day I would get married. However, I chose a different lifestyle, always eager to explore what was different. I was constantly flooded with thoughts that God hadn't given me this life only to get married.

I was in seventh grade when I dropped out of school because of an incident that changed my life forever. In my teacher's absence, I role played being a teacher, standing on her chair and delivering a speech. I was caught by my teacher who then went on to beat me relentlessly in front of the entire class, abusing and humiliating me while my classmates looked on and made fun of me. I was deeply hurt and cried inconsolably. I felt suicidal and refused to return to school.

My parents tried to convince me to enrol in another school - I blatantly refused to do so. However, I never stopped studying. I self-studied without the aid of any tuition. This encouraged me to open my own school in the courtyard of my home. I made home visits in my village and other villages nearby, distributing pamphlets I had made announcing the free education I would provide.

Irrespective of how many visits I made, no one was ready to join my school as I was just thirteen years old. I didn't allow this to discourage me as I didn't want any child to experience what I did in school. I promised myself to make education interesting for my students while ensuring they felt respected, loved and cared for, unlike how I felt in school. I got my break when one student joined my school. My classes were held outdoors with only a few books. Summer classes were under the sun and winter classes under blankets but when it rained, we had to abandon our classes.

By age sixteen, I completed grade twelve and started working as a receptionist for a telecom franchise which paid $15 a month and it was with this $15 that I started purchasing stationery and other items for my school. I continued working and teaching. My classes were always conducted in my courtyard.

I completed my Bachelors in Arts as a private student in 2008, landing an assistant manager's position with a Pakistan Telecommunication Company. I joined social media in 2011 and started sharing details of my school on Facebook. Then I went on to become a volunteer admin for the World-Wide Women's Facebook page who also recommended I join World Pulse. It was there that I started posting my story and that of my students not knowing the extent to which I was being noticed as I focused only on the fact that my story was being shared amongst an international community.

However in 2013, a competition was held amongst women from 196 countries. We were asked to write three blog posts on how we use technology for our work. I was delighted to learn that I had been shortlisted. I was honoured to be interviewed by the CEO of World Pulse, Lynn Syms herself and at the end, I was asked to share any questions I had. I jokingly replied, "When will you announce that I have won?"

Fifteen days later, in a state of utter shock which left me trembling, I learnt that I had won the award. The prize money of $20,000 changed my life. Using this, I bought a small piece of land and had two rooms built while we also purchased school supplies. All the long and hard days of working 18 hours had finally culminated into this - we were eventually able to put a roof over our students' heads after fourteen years of running the school in a courtyard.

I have taught thousands of girls over two decades and empowered even more. I was approached via social media by Channel News Asia Singapore who wanted to make a film on my story. Initially, I didn't take them seriously but they kept contacting me until I relented. 'Flight of the Falcons' is my story which went on to win a Gold Medal at the New York Film Festival in 2016.

I currently run two schools with 200 registered students who receive twelve years of free education while we also support skills training of 400 women annually. We are a registered nonprofit and our students take exams through certified platforms.

Our students go on to college and university, graduating as teachers, nurses, estheticians, tailors, HR managers, to name just a few. They are strong and independent while they are also safe from child marriage, honour killing and rape. I was honoured to receive the Bioners Change Makers Award in 2015, the Outstanding Performance Award by Isaac TV and eternal life ministries of Pakistan International in 2018.

I continue to keep my promise of treating my students with love, respect, care and compassion. In light of this, I would like to share the plight of a young nine-year-old student of mine who was severely burnt in an accident recently. She was cooking dinner for her young siblings when disaster struck. A fire left her with second and third degree burns on the front and back of her torso. Her parents locked her up in a dark room with no air conditioning, treatment or care for an entire month only because she is a girl.

Due to the Eid school vacations, I only heard about her plight a month after the incident. After quite a struggle with her parents and with the help of friends, I was able to admit the little girl to a private hospital. Initially, no hospital would admit her for treatment due to the severity of her injuries including continuous blood loss and pus oozing from her wounds. However, with the support of friends in USA and connections in Pakistan we facilitated her admission into a private hospital. She needed her own private room because her wounds were open and infected with a deadly bacteria which was highly contagious.

Her treatment continues but she still requires a lot of financial support for her medical costs. To learn more about her and how you can help with her recovery and would be grateful for any donations.

SISTER ZEPH

FOUNDER OF ZEPHANIAH FREE EDUCATION

learnmoreabout.info/free_education

Sister Zeph is the founder of Zephaniah Free Education, a registered nonprofit which provides free education to girls in Pakistan. Zephaniah Free Education currently runs two schools with over two hundred registered students who receive twelve years of free education while the nonprofit also focuses on skill training of four hundred women educating them in trades such as esthetics, tailoring and art.

Sister Zeph has a few accolades to her name including the Bioneers Change makers award, Outstanding performance award by Isaac TV, eternal life ministries of Pakistan International and she was also awarded the Lynn Syms Global prize. Channel News Asia Singapore produced a movie on her life story, Flight of the Falcons which won a Gold Medal at the New York film festival in 2016. Sister Zeph's goal is to safeguard every girl in Pakistan from child marriage, honour killing, violence, rape and equip them to be strong and independent.

"As women, we often feel guilty and selfish for wanting to have it all and put ourselves first. It is vital that we shift our mind-space and start giving importance to ourselves. When we achieve a balance, everything else is possible."

- Bridget Zyka -

MY JOURNEY TO SELF LOVE AND HAPPINESS

My story begins back when I was growing up. As a young girl, I was always confident and full of myself. The term used to describe me was "tomboy." I was into everything that kept me active and loved being outdoors every day. Doubts about my appearance and weight suddenly crept into my psyche and emotions when I was a teenager. I became more aware of myself and what people thought of me easily. I wasn't comfortable in my own skin anymore. Suddenly, I wanted to be more perfect than I already was.

My main issue with weight and trying to control it, started at University. Somehow, when you are away from home, you're not quite sure how to shop for, prepare and eat healthy meals so you end up grabbing what is accessible. On a tight budget and time constraints, it did become difficult and I found myself living off student meals. I ate weird combinations of food and for the first month I literally ate cheese sandwiches most of the time.

After completing University and saving enough money from my first few jobs, I decided to go travelling and explore the world. I had always been driven to explore because I was curious to see more of the world. Even at that age, I felt that life was too short and therefore craved niche adventures. Something inside of me was curious about what was there beyond the world that I was living in. I wanted to know how others lived. I wanted to know what was out there to see and do that was different. I knew that I would never be satisfied with what was available in my own surroundings. To me, it is as if my soul had already come to know that there was more for me to experience and I instinctively knew that the choices I needed to make had to be ones that would propel me into a life out of the ordinary.

Once I'd moved to New Zealand, I started to develop health issues that were indirectly related to my weight and my lack of self worth. I was feeling trapped as I was in a career I wasn't enjoying. I was attracting toxic relationships and using food as a crutch. It was the one thing I thought that I had control over while everything else seemed to be spinning out of control. I was going out every weekend and drinking until 6am, refusing to go home at a reasonable hour. The worse I felt about myself the worse I felt about my body. It seemed to me that when I ate and drank, I was eating and drinking my feelings, expressing what I felt about myself through food, eating down the lump in my throat and silent tears with every swallow I made. I was a growing shell, getting larger but totally empty on the inside. I existed on the seashore and rode some waves and then remained still for others. What I really wanted, if I had to be completely honest, was for my shell to liven up. Because somewhere inside my empty depths, I knew that something good and wholesome was amiss and that when it did return to me, I'd no longer be just that lonely shell on the seashore.

I eventually sought out the help of a Naturopath. I had been diagnosed as pre-diabetic and thanks to the advice I was able to reverse it. I started to take care of my body and made better decisions for myself going forward. I took care to eat well, exercise more, meditate and relax when needed and pay attention to what my body was communicating to me. I paid attention when I was grocery shopping. I made healthier choices. I moved schedules around and got rid of toxic living habits to make way for wholesome practises to enter my life. By that time, I had moved to London and was finally happy with myself and my body. As a direct result, I lost all the weight without thinking about it. I was happy and was making decisions from a place of love. I was also practicing Intuitive eating without realising the name for it. I was working with my body and not against it. I was feeding my body and soul with experiences I enjoyed. I revelled in being able to be in control of my thoughts and feelings again. Everybody noticed the changes, not only in my looks, but in my temperament. How I interacted with people on a daily basis changed from aggression and impatience to genuine happiness and interest in others.

Now I am in a happy place and am very mindful of what I am doing. I treat my body holistically, making sure every part of me is taken care of. I find ways that inspire me to do more to look after my body and mind in a healthy way. I make the time to enjoy activities that light me up and set my soul on fire. I am no longer just that growing sea shell on the seashore. I am making conscious decisions about my life every day.

After everything I have been through, I have made it my mission to show other women how to practice self-love. When we truly love and respect our bodies, it has a 'domino effect' on the rest of our lives. We can achieve anything we set our minds to. We can have the perfect career, set up that business, find the partner of our dreams and it all starts from loving ourselves enough and wanting to make those vital changes for ourselves first.

BRIDGET ZYKA

THE BODY POSITIVITY COACH

instagram.com/thebodypositivitycoach

Bridget Zyka, The Body Positivity Coach had it all on paper. She had a high flying IT job, was smarter than even she gave herself credit for, and was rearing to make things happen in her life but something was amiss. It was the need to find inner happiness and joy, brought on by body weight challenges, she was not equipped to handle at the time.

Her body was crying out for love. She abused it in all the wrong ways. She decided to start loving her body, turned her life around. She decided to stop hiding and start shining. When she did that, she stumbled on her new path and now helps others achieve exactly what she did, which is to become comfortably awesome.

TEAM - RISE

A big thank you to these incredible experts that were working on this book.

NASREEN VARIYAWA - EDITOR

PRITPAL MATHARU - BOOK DESIGN

PARUL AGRAWAL - LAUNCH EXPERT

NASREEN VARIYAWA

IGNITO EDITING AND
GHOSTWRITING CONSULTING

nvariyawa@yahoo.com

*It gives me great pleasure to submit this message for
'Rise: In Pursuit of Empowerment'. Sabine's dream to publish a
book spurred me on to use my skills and talents to help her and
the other co-authors reach their goals.*

*An English teacher, author, ghostwriter and editor by profession,
each of the co-authors touched my life in a positive way. Through
their stories, each one of them has brought home the message that
no matter what happens in our lives, we have the ability to rise
above it and ensure that we survive and thrive. Above all, each of
them is a brave star for sharing their stories and baring their souls
to ensure, that just like me, you too have been touched positively.*

*We look forward to the forthcoming editions from 'Reach for
Greatness' and we encourage you to share your stories with us.
So, get those fingers walking and your thoughts talking...*

"Keep smiling, keep shining, keep rising."

PRITPAL MATHARU

GRAPHIC DESIGNER

letscre8.tv

Pritpal is a Brand Creation Strategist that helps businesses turn their visions into a cohesive and inspirational brand identity. Pritpal tends to work closely with his clients to achieve high end designs that are bespoke, innovative and unique. He always strives to research current trends, using humour, creativity and endless imagination.

He has been instrumental in all creative aspects for the book. His mission was to produce highly impactful and stunning graphics. Spanning from designing the front cover to interior spreads and social media visuals.

Inspired by every story told, he created an imagery of stars that showcase women who have risen above their challenges. Hence the star theme throughout the book was introduced.

"Overall I'm very pleased with the end result, giving every story character, energy and purpose."

PARUL AGRAWAL

AUTHOR, PODCAST HOST, BESTSELLER LAUNCH EXPERT

parulagrawal.com

Parul Agrawal holds a double Master's in Engineering from Arizona State University (ASU); worked as a Research Scientist at ASU and Engineer for Intel Corporation. In an effort to help others address major medical issues and live more healthily, she pursued holistic studies and wrote "Juicing for Healthier Families"- an International Bestseller in multiple categories. The book's phenomenal success resulted in her being featured in major publications like the Huffington Post, Thrive Global, Forbes and was a guest on ABC Arizona.

Parul has not only continued her success as an author and business woman, but she has paid-it-forward, by helping over 100 writers become bestselling authors. She is the founder of an International Publishing Platform where she helps thought leaders in the areas of health, wellness and consciousness write their books, achieve bestseller authority status, and land in mainstream media.

CHARITIES

Through this book we are supporthing charities that will make
a difference to many other lives. We would be grateful for any dontions.

ZEPHANIAH - FREE EDUCATION

MENDING 1000 HEARTS

ZEPHANIAH FREE EDUCATION

learnmoreabout.info/free_education

We provide 12 years of free schooling to the most disadvantaged in rural Pakistan, where our literacy rate is 172nd in the world behind Nigeria.

We also provide free skills training to hundreds of women every year free of charge. We teach IT, Computer literacy, stitching, self defense, health classes and more.

Our work also helps keep children out of child labour and child marriage. It prevents young girls often as young as thirteen from child marriage and having children at an early age.

MENDING 1000 HEARTS

learnmoreabout.info/mendinghearts

*The 'Mending 1000 Hearts Campaign' is championed
by 'Mending Kids' long-term donor and volunteer
Naomi Carmona-Morshead. All donations will go towards
life-saving cardiac surgeries and procedures through
Mending Kids' programs around the world.*

*Mending Kids gives sick children life-saving surgical care, while
advancing education and training towards medical sufficiency
in their communities. Since 1993, we have mended thousands of
children in over 64 countries, including the US.*

RISE

Rise for the heart that was torn
Rise for the war that you fought
Rise for those that let you down
Rise 'cos you didn't drown, Rise!

Rise because it is you who bled
Rise because of the tears you shed
Rise 'cos you're a beacon of hope
Rise 'cos you're the light that glows, Rise!

Rise 'cos you loved them so
Rise 'cos they didn't know
Rise 'cos you didn't lose
Rise 'cos you weren't a snooze, Rise!

Rise for the integrity you learnt
Rise 'cos life left you burnt
Rise for the roads that were rough
Rise 'cos you proved you were tough, Rise!

Rise 'cos of the stories you tell
Rise 'cos of the lessons you spell
Rise 'cos you're the icon of strength
Rise 'cos you refused to bend, Rise!

★ *Rise heroes rise!* ★

Rise for the road ahead
Rise 'cos you're alive, not dead
Rise for the goals that are bigger
Rise for the desire to be better, Rise!

Rise 'cos your role is vital
Rise 'cos you're teaching survival
Rise for the path you took
Rise for your new book, Rise!

Rise 'cos you worked so hard
Rise 'cos you hold the trumpcard
Rise as you continue to thrive
Rise 'cos you do more than survive, Rise!

Rise for the talent that you have
Rise for the ship that you drive
Rise for the doors you now open
Rise for the path that you've chosen, Rise!

Rise for daring to dream
Rise for the vision you've weaved
Rise for daring to try
For reaching new heights, Rise!

★ *by Nasreen Variyawa* ★

RISE

In Pursuit of Empowerment

....

WANT TO BE AN AUTHOR IN THE NEXT SERIES?

....

We are constantly looking for inspirational stories to be published for the next series of books. If you are interested in becoming a published author please apply by following the link below:

REACH
FOR GREATNESS

★ www.learnmoreabout.info/becomeanauthor ★